The train sweeps on past
The storm beats on by
The fight rages fast
And dark grows the sky.

The shells of sin are shattering
In fierce & deathly "bangs"!
The few true ones are shattering
Before the serpent's fangs.

The biting snow is racing
With the cold & cutting sleet
The few "right" ones are facing
A battle few can meet!

The only hope for us now
Is from Christ our Lord & King
The answer (all are asking How?)
Is Him — So let us sing!

Yet
But who lies in this lonely yard,
Where only Birds come too?
Asleep least the their bodies their souls
Are with God.
Up in the Heavens so blue.

Yet hear on earth their bodies are dear
To us who are left behind
And even their frames in their graves
seem so near,
And they helps us more — to be king

Yet my mind loves to rome
To that graveyard back there.
Ti there are loved ones are — back home
And when we remember that heart—
rending care
I love to think that their bodies are there
In that small friendly graveyard
back home.

"Where I was born"

FOOTPRINTS *of a* PILGRIM

Footprints of a Pilgrim

THE LIFE AND LOVES of
RUTH BELL GRAHAM

WORD PUBLISHING
NASHVILLE
A Thomas Nelson Company

FOOTPRINTS OF A PILGRIM

Cover photos:
Ruth and Billy Graham with growing family—
Gigi, Anne, Bunny (Ruth), and Franklin. Ned has yet to arrive.

Ruth kissing another missionary child, Gay Currie,
who is still living in Black Mountain, North Carolina.

For more information about Ruth Bell Graham, her books, and the
"Footprints of a Pilgrim" reader's theatre production, contact:
www.ruthbellgraham.com
www.wordpublishing.com.

The majority of photos are from the personal collection of
Ruth Bell Graham and photographic attributions have been lost.
Many photographs were provided by Virginia Somerville and Russ Busby and
the Billy Graham Evangelistic Association (especially on pages 48, 49, and 76).
Also, additional photos were provided courtesy of Charles Massey, Jr. (148, 149),
Donna Campbell and UNC-TV (125, 152, 155, 166),
Stephen Griffith (19, 143, 167,168), Julie Tchividjian (158-160),
the Wheaton College Archives (62, 63), and Montreat College (113, 75).

Scripture quotations used in this book are from the following sources:
The King James Version of the Bible (KJV).
The New King James Version (NKJV), copyright ©1979, 1980, 1982,
Thomas Nelson, Inc., Publishers.
The Revised Standard Version of the Bible (RSV), ©1952, 1971 by the Division of
Christian Education of the National Council of the Churches of Christ in the USA.

Library of Congress Cataloging-in-Publication Data

Graham, Ruth Bell.
    Footprints of a pilgrim/by Ruth Bell Graham.
        p. cm.
    ISBN 0-8499-1675-5 (hardcover)
    1. Graham, Ruth Bell. 2. Baptists—United States—Biography. 3. Evangelists' spouses—United States—Biography. 4. Spouses of clergy—United States—Biography. 5. Children of missionaries—China—Biography. 6. Graham, Billy, 1918– I. Title.

BX6495.G666 A3 2001
269'.2'092—dc21
[B]   2001017685

Printed in the United States of America

01 02 03 04 05 PHX 9 8 7 6 5 4 3 2 1

Acknowledgments

There were many people who helped in the process of making this book. The idea began in 1997 with Stephen Griffith, who nurtured and managed the process until its completion. My daughter Gigi Tchividjian also has helped navigate the book through its growing pains. Equally necessary to the project's success have been Bill, my children, siblings (especially Virginia Sommerville), the household and Montreat office staff, friends, and neighbors. I've also appreciated assistance given by Lamb's Players Theatre, Robert and Deborah Smyth, Dave and Beth Heath, Kerry Meads, Jeannette Clift George, The Ruth and Billy Graham Children's Health Center Foundation, Donna Campbell and UNC-TV, Jeff Johnson, Steve West, Lorraine Griffith, Victoria Griffith, Patricia Cornwell, Jan Karon, Barbara Bush, Virginia Sommerville, Russ Busby and the Billy Graham Evangelistic Association, Joey Paul and the staff at Word Publishing, Dwight Baker at Baker Book House, Chris Gilbert and the staff at Uttley/DouPonce DesignWorks, Mindy Clinard at Montreat College, and David Malone at the Wheaton College Archives. There are others whom I know I've forgotten and I apologize.

Ruth Bell Graham

LITTLE PINEY COVE
MARCH 1, 2001

Contents

One of the things I love
about her poetry is that it is
so visual. She can take me out
of doors just like that.

JAN KARON

Foreword: The Hallmark of Greatness

R uth Graham's work possesses what I believe to be the hallmark of greatness: It is intensely personal, yet also distinctly universal. For example, I urge you to demonstrate the truth of this observation by reading her poetry. Read it alone, hugging it to yourself. Then, read it aloud to your family, as Charles Dickens's devoted readers eagerly read his work aloud to their families. The depth and nuance of her passion will not only thrill and move you privately, it will come alive in the imaginations of your loved ones in ways that have the power to touch.

Since reading poetry at all, much less aloud, is hardly our national pastime, you may wonder: Is Ruth Graham's poetry, like the stuff you read in school, too hard, too obscure, too odd to grapple with? Never! In her work, you'll hear a voice you may sometimes recognize as your own—that of a wife, a mother, a sweetheart, a child; a woman, an adventurer, a visionary and even, occasionally, a doubter. Ruth Graham has many voices, and she doesn't try to hide or disguise even one of them.

Would we dare to be so open, so transparent, if we were wife of a man who's known and loved the world over? Ruth Graham has dared. She has dared, however, not because she wanted to or thought she should, but because she couldn't help it.

PHOTO FROM RUTH'S PASSPORT.

Her poems are dear to my heart. I've read them alone—and to others—for a long time now. It is always a joy to sit by this poet's laughing fire or to walk with her through the crisp, loud leaves of fall, watching mist curl among the hills of Little Piney Cove.

I've had the privilege and delight of meeting Ruth Graham in person, of sitting with her and Dr. Graham by their fireside while they held hands like teenage sweethearts. It is her work, however, that enables me to say that I've not only met Ruth Graham, but know her.

—JAN KARON

Rosegate 2001

Introduction: The Itching

GIGI GRAHAM TCHIVIDJIAN

Gigi, what is this thing you organized about Mother that will be taking place in Asheville Monday night?" Daddy's voice boomed over the telephone. "I hear that no one will attend and that it is going to embarrass a lot of people, including Mother."

He continued, "I think we should cancel it."

I felt sick. We had worked so hard to pull this together. The theater had been secured months before, tickets had been issued, actors had arrived from California and Texas, musicians had been lined up, and catering had been arranged.

It was not your usual type of event. Not many people in our area had been exposed to readers' theater productions, and I could understand that Daddy didn't have a clue as to what this was all about.

I did my best to remain calm and tried to explain the event.

At the end of the telephone conversation, I said, "Daddy, the last thing we want to do is embarrass anyone. If you really want us to refund the tickets and cancel the production, I will do my best, but it is a bit late."

"Well, honey, let me talk to some of my people and get back to you."

I was shaking. I was leaving in the morning for Missouri, where I would be speaking to a women's conference. I still had to pack, prepare a talk, and deal with this unexpected turn of events.

A few moments later, the phone rang again. "Gigi, what is this thing you are doing in Asheville?" my brother Franklin asked. "Poetry? No one goes to hear poetry, Gigi. Don't you understand that this is going to embarrass Mama, Gigi? And you don't want to do that, do you now, Gigi? No one will come to such a thing, and if no one shows up it will be an embarrassment to all concerned, including Daddy, Mama, as well as the Children's Health Center."[1]

Again I tried to explain, but of all people, I didn't think that Franklin would be able to understand or grasp the idea behind this unusual event. Neither he nor Daddy has been known to understand my mother's work. Nor did they have a clue as to the professional nature of this production and the honor it would bring to Mother.

"Gigi," Franklin continued, "I think that you should cancel this event. In fact, I will call and cancel it for you, if it would help. We don't want Mama to be embarrassed, do we?"

I sighed. I was tired physically and emotionally, and I had a plane to catch the next morning. *Maybe*, I thought, *we should just cancel it and forget about the whole idea.*

I thought about why we had organized this event in the first place. We hadn't planned on a sold-out crowd, but the theater was going to be almost full. We didn't really care about the crowd; we were doing this for Mother.

Mother's writing is very dear to her heart because she has spent many lonely nights sharing her thoughts and feelings, baring her soul with pen and paper.

During the publishing process of Mother's book of collected poems, her friend Stephen Griffith, who helps put her manuscripts in publishable form, said that after spending months on this book, he came to believe that anyone who wanted to know

---

[1] We had planned to give all of the proceeds to the Ruth and Billy Graham Children's Health Center, which is a part of Mission St. Joseph Medical Center in Asheville, North Carolina.

Ruth Graham and her relationship with her husband, children, and friends was missing a great deal if they ignored her poetry.

Personally, I have always thought that Mother reveals her personality in her prose, but she reveals her heart and soul in her poetry.

But because poetry is often overlooked, we came up with the idea of putting together a professional readers' theater production of Mother's life story told in her own words through her prose and poetry. In this way, the content of her poems would be illustrated in the context of her life story.

Stephen Griffith worked long and hard to make sure that this evening would be a success. So, needless to say, when I told him we might have to cancel the event, he was beside himself.

While I was waiting to hear if the event would be canceled, the telephone rang again.

"Hello, honey, it's Mother."

"Where are you?" I asked.

"I sneaked off to my room to call you," she replied. "I don't know what has gotten into Daddy and Franklin. Why do they think this event is going to embarrass anyone?"

"Mother, I don't know. But if you want me to cancel it, I will."

"Heavens no, honey," came her quick reply.

I called Daddy back just to check. He agreed with Mother that we should proceed. I called Steve and told him to keep going—full steam ahead.

I had to smile as I packed my bags for Missouri, where I was to speak to women on the subject of serenity. I thought to myself, *God really does have a sense of humor.*

That evening, Mother was preparing for bed. But when Mother is upset, her head begins to itch, and after all that had transpired, it itched terribly. She couldn't get to sleep but remembered that she had something in one of the bathroom drawers for itching.

She got up, found it, and rubbed it all over her scalp. The itching subsided, and she soon fell asleep. In the morning, she awoke only to find her hair standing straight up all over her head like a hedgehog.

She looked at the tube of itching cream and discovered that she had rubbed Preparation H all over her head. It took her three shampooings and an application of dishwashing liquid to get it out.

The program went on as scheduled. On the evening of April 5, 1998, we arrived at the lovely, intimate Diana Wortham Theater at Pack Place in Asheville, greeted by music from the hammered dulcimer and flute (Lisa and Jerry Reid Smith), a beautiful buffet of Chinese food and specialties (from Mother's favorite restaurant, Tong Sings), and a gallery of original paintings by Richard Jesse Watson (from Mother's book *One Wintry Night* and other books Richard has illustrated).

The theater was packed, and to everyone's delight, the event was a huge success. Several times during the production, Daddy took my hand and tightly squeezed it. He was very moved.

One skeptical friend (my father's close associate, T. W. Wilson), who was sure that the production would be a flop, told me afterward, "Gigi, I fell in love with your mother the moment I met her more than fifty years ago, but tonight I fell in love with her all over again."

In fact, this special evening led to many people asking if the program was going to be repeated. So in celebration of Mother's eightieth birthday, a lovely dinner was held in her honor at the historic Grove Park Inn in Asheville, North Carolina, on May 30, 2000. In planning the evening's program, we could think of no better way to honor her life than to present once again *Footprints of a Pilgrim.* Everyone was enthralled by the life of this small, feisty, humorous, intelligent, deeply spiritual pilgrim of faith.

Now it is with great pleasure and deep emotion that I offer you, through these pages, with added stories, interviews, and photos, the privilege of walking hand in hand with this pilgrim as she retraces a few of the footsteps of her life.

THE 80TH BIRTHDAY CELEBRATION AT GROVE PARK INN, ASHEVILLE, NORTH CAROLINA

RUTH GRAHAM, WITH DAUGHTER GIGI, NOVELIST PATRICIA CORNWELL AND ANDIE MACDOWELL AT THE PRESS CONFERENCE FOR THE 80TH BIRTHDAY CELEBRATION.

The Paint of Words

THE BELLS IN CHINA: (FROM LEFT TO RIGHT) THE ELDEST DAUGHTER
ROSA, VIRGINIA, JR. (AS SHE WAS LOVINGLY CALLED BY HER FATHER AND
MOTHER), NELSON BELL, VIRGINIA BELL, AND RUTH. ONE BROTHER,
LEMUEL NELSON BELL, JR., WAS BORN BETWEEN RUTH AND VIRGINIA BUT
DIED AT THE AGE OF ELEVEN MONTHS. BROTHER CLAYTON WAS BORN
SOON AFTER THIS PICTURE.

Anyone who wants to know
Ruth Graham and her relationship
with her husband, children,
and friends is missing a great deal
if they ignore her poetry.

STEPHEN GRIFFITH

I love the paint of words

the arc of phrase

the dance of metaphor

alive upon the page

Bits and pieces

Bits

and Pieces.

From Journals

Letters

Notebooks

Thoughts

Prayers

Observations

Sketches

The poetry of a lifetime

The footprints of a pilgrim—

I can't remember when I wasn't scribbling something.

I jot things down when I can't sleep

or I'm too tired

or I need to reflect on friends

family,

frustrations.

funny moments,

Notebook upon notebook

A storehouse of memories . . .

A bit cluttered perhaps,

THE PACK-RAT'S ATTIC AT
LITTLE PINEY COVE.

THE END PAPERS AND THE DIARY SHOWN ON THIS AND THE FOLLOWING
PAGES WERE KEPT BY RUTH AT THE AGE OF TEN. THE DRAWING ON THE
ENDPAGES IS THE COMPOUND IN CHINA, WHICH HOUSED THE HOSPITAL
AND MISSIONARY QUARTERS.

I admit it.

I'm a pack rat.

With a "proclivity for

disorganization," some have said.

But that's completely untrue—I just

hate to throw anything away.

Sometimes I wrote to capture a moment

or reflect on a thought

Sometimes, I wrote because I had to.

It was write or develop an ulcer.

I chose to write.

Now, I know how some of you might feel about poetry, so I

want to make myself perfectly clear . . .

My poems were never intended for publication.

Or recitation.

I wrote them

for myself.

It was a pale blue dawn
dewy
and still.
Three golden clouds
stretched thin
above the black hill.
The purpling coves

awash in mist
slowly turned
to amethyst.
It was a pale blue dawn . . .

They come and go so quickly
Spring and Fall . . .
as if they had not really
come at all.
Perhaps
we could not take
too much of beauty,
breath-catching glory,
ecstasy without relief;
and so . . .
God made them
brief.

Blinking
back the tears
I'm thinking,
may just clear
the heart for sight:
as windshield wipers
help us
on a stormy,
windswept night.

THE ORIGINAL CABIN (AND DETAIL) AT
LITTLE PINEY COVE. THE SMALL
HOLLY TREE IN FRONT OF THE CABIN
TOWERS OVER THE CABIN TODAY.

Piney Cove

Ruth McCue Bell

Memories in
verse
Written By R. M. B.
All save the first
Dares it
Mysterious Hidden
Secrent

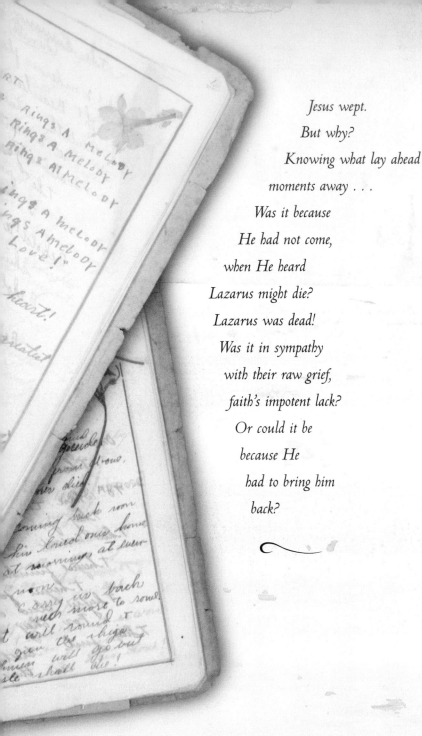

Jesus wept.
But why?
Knowing what lay ahead
moments away . . .
Was it because
He had not come,
when He heard
Lazarus might die?
Lazarus was dead!
Was it in sympathy
with their raw grief,
faith's impotent lack?
Or could it be
because He
had to bring him
back?

It is no nightingale tonight,
no whippoorwill,
enchanting pale
twilight
with singing on the hill
for us . . .
only the limpid frogs,
hatched in the damp
someplace,
raising their hallelujah
chorus
loud!
and I am touched
with grace.

Early Life in China

The rickshaw was the main mode of transportation from the hospital to Shanghai. This photo shows Ruth, Virginia, Virginia, Jr., Rosa, and Dr. Bell, waiting to begin their journey to Shanghai.

How could she know that this

was her training period . . .

her boot camp?

Preparation for her future.

GIGI GRAHAM TCHIVIDJIAN

"Children of the Heavenly Father,
Safely to his bosom gather" . . .

This pilgrim's journey began in the Year of the Monkey—1920—in Quingjiang, China, the second daughter of medical missionaries Nelson and Virginia Bell.

Many Chinese pitied these "foreign devils," who now had "two nuisances" in tow. Many did not trust Western doctors. They were "monsters who made medicine from dead baby eyes and turned Chinese bones into gold for themselves."

A missionary doctor was sought out only as a last resort.

RUTH

NELSON BELL, RUTH, ROSA, VIRGINIA BELL

(BACKGROUND: RUTH AND ROSA)

A WOMAN WEIGHING 180 POUNDS ARRIVED AT THE
HOSPITAL one day, pushing her stomach ahead of her in a
wheelbarrow. After my father removed her tumor, she
weighed 90 pounds.

Another time a local peasant came to the mission hospital because his broken ankle had fused with his foot,
pointing backward.

My father—a skilled surgeon—did everything . . .
from removing cataracts, to filling teeth, to amputations . . . creating
prosthetics out of beams of wood.

He even made house calls on a black Harley-Davidson. He'd ride fifty miles into the countryside with a sidecar to boot.

And though he cared for people's physical health, what
mattered most to him was their spiritual health. He wrote himself
a reminder . . . on a ragged slip of paper (Daddy was a scribbler,
too) and kept it under the glass on his roll-top desk . . .

Love,
Joy,
Peace,
Long-suffering,
Gentleness,
Goodness,
Faithfulness,
Meekness,
And Self-Control.

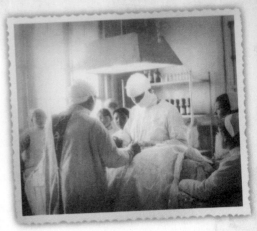

DR. BELL PERFORMING SURGERY AT THE
LOVE AND MERCY HOSPITAL.

RUTH AND ROSA WITH THEIR FATHER A
MOTHER IN THE BLACK HARLE

(BACKGROUND: THE WOMAN'S HOSPITAL AND
ADMINISTRATIVE BUILDING, WHICH HOUSED THE
OPERATING ROOM, CHAPEL, AND OFFICES OF THE
LOVE AND MERCY HOSPITAL.)

Growing up I had a nanny.

"She's a homely old soul," my mother once commented, which aroused in us children an indignant response.

Huh!?

Then we looked more objectively.

Her nose was unusually broad and flat, and there was a mole on the side of it.

Her eyes were little slits with short eyelashes, framed by laugh wrinkles.

Her mouth was wide and kind.

A peasant's face.

A pleasant peasant's face.

Mother was right.

She was a homely old soul.

But what did that matter; she was so loving, I would have sworn her beautiful.

Her name was Wang Nai Nai.

We called her amah.

We children loved her. Everyone did.

If I close my eyes I can see her sitting on a low stool in the upstairs back bedroom, singing . . . her hand-bound Chinese hymnal open in her hands . . .

"There is a fountain filled with blood
Drawn from Immanuel's veins,
And sinners plunged beneath that flood
Lose all their guilty stains" . . .

Ruth Graham on Reading as a Child

I was born and raised in China, and books were just a part of our life. We didn't have television, fortunately, which was a great blessing.

In the evening was family time, and after Daddy was finished making his rounds at the hospital, the men would take turns reading—Sir Walter Scott, Uncle Remus, etc.—and the women would do handiwork. Mother taught us to crochet and embroider, things like that.

Reading was a very early love in my life.

To my innocent young mind, she was the picture of a saintly soul at worship. It was years later, when I was considered "old enough to be told such things," that I learned how meaningful the old hymn was to her. When young, Wang Nai Nai and her husband had been "procurers." This was a time in China when baby girls were not generally wanted. So the shady business of buying unwanted girls to sell to "certain houses" in Shanghai was a road to easy money.

"The dying thief rejoiced to see
That fountain in his day,
And there may I, though vile as he,
Wash all my sins away."

Then one day, Wang Nai Nai heard from a missionary about a God who hated her sin but loved her unconditionally. She could become a child of that God if she would accept the forgiveness He offered her through His Son, Jesus.

It was as straightforward and simple as that.

Of such fabric, God weaves some of His choicest saints.

WANG NAI NAI WITH
ROSA AND RUTH.

DURING MUCH OF MY YOUTH, CHINA WAS LOCKED in a bloody civil war between Nationalist Chinese leader Chiang Kai-shek and Communist rebels. All around were marching troops . . .

mysterious deaths and kidnappings,

bandits in the night.

Gunfire,

air raids,

dangers all around,

but China was our home.

RUTH AND ROSA ON THE STREET IN HOUSTON, TEXAS WHILE ON A RARE FURLOUGH.

RUTH AND VIRGINIA WITH THE DOG TARBABY, OR TB, AS HE CAME TO BE KNOWN.

BACKGROUND: THE WOMEN'S WARD OF THE LOVE AND MERCY HOSPITAL.

As a young girl, I tried to keep diaries.

I began each one optimistically on the first of January—but they flickered out shortly after. One entry read, "I found a baby mouse today, but it bit me and died."

When my pet rabbit died, I did what I did with any one of my many pets that died . . . I planned a funeral complete with hymns and eulogies.

The little white rabbit was buried in my animal cemetery near the sand pile along with those who had gone on before—canaries, pigeons, ducks, turtles, kittens, guinea pigs. Every day I dug up the rabbit's grave to see how he was getting along. The last time I saw him . . . he was green.

I had a habit of picking up any dead animal I stumbled upon. Whether it was a pet or not, I figured it deserved a funeral.

My mother abruptly put an end to this practice . . . when she noticed a rather rank smell coming from a closet one day and discovered a dead bird I had forgotten in my sweater pocket.

Yuck.

Ruth Graham on Her Childhood Journal

We didn't have notebooks in China, so I got some wallpaper and made the back and front cover and then got some of Daddy's stationery from the hospital, cut off the masthead, and made the inside pages.

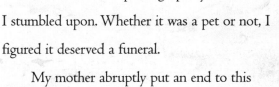

I also enjoyed drawing.

"Our Ruth," my father wrote to his mother, "has real artistic talent. For a long time we knew she was clever with drawing, but recently shows remarkable talent. . . . But it has never been a talent I have especially desired for a child of mine."

Drawings by Ruth.

I STRUGGLED—TO FIND MY PLACE, my niche, my own sense of beauty.

I admired the almond eyes and ebony hair and the graceful manner of the Chinese women in their colorful silks and satins. Dressed in secondhand clothing rummaged from the missionary barrel, I felt awkward by comparison.

I started writing poems. . . . This was one of my first:

It isn't your gold or silver,
your talents great or small,
your voice, or your gift of drawing,
or the crowd you go with at all:
it isn't your friends or pastimes,
your looks or your clothes so gay;
it isn't your home or family,
or even the things you say;
it isn't your choice of amusements,
it isn't the life you lead,
it isn't the thing you prize the most,
or the books you like to read;
no, it isn't the things you have, dear,
or the things you like to do,
the Master is searching deeper . . .
He seeks not yours, but you.

It's your heart that Jesus longs for;
your will to be made His own
with self on the cross forever,
and Jesus alone on the throne.

ROSA AND RUTH WITH HSU YIN,
THE DAUGHTER OF WANG NAI NAI.

ROSA AND RUTH

"Jesus loves me this I know" . . .

China is veritably a country of graves . . .

In every direction outside the mission compound, the expanse of land was interrupted by thousands of tan, conical grave mounds. They were kept clear of grass and weeds by family caretakers who feared the wrath of the ancestors they worshiped.

In this land of too many people and too little food, thousands of acres of farmland were sown only with bones and superstition.

Look o'er the fields about you—
riveted, hilled with graves;
no one can count the number
of those who perished as slaves;
slaves to the sin they were born in,
knowing not God or His Light;
died without God's great salvation,
died in the darkness of night.

Look o'er the people about you—
faces so furrowed with care,
lined and hardened by sorrow
sin has placed on them there;
think of the evil they live in,
hopes none and joys so few;
love them, pray for them, win them,
lest they should perish, too.

CHINESE GRAVES OUTSIDE THE HOSPITAL COMPOUND,
NEXT TO THE DEFENSE WALL TO THE CITY.

Like a shadow declining
swiftly away . . . away . . .
like the dew of the morning
gone with the heat of the day;
like the wind in the treetops,
like a wave of the sea,
so are our lives on earth when seen
in light of eternity.

BACKGROUND: THE PHOENIX WAS A PRIVATE LAUNCH LOANED FOR ONE TRIP
ONLY. OTHER LAUNCHES WERE USED FOR THE MISSIONARIES AND HOSPITAL
PERSONNEL TO TRAVEL UP AND DOWN THE GRAND CHANNEL.

AT THIRTEEN, I WAS TO LEAVE HOME . . . to sail away, to what is now North Korea, to go to the Piang Yang Foreign School. I didn't want to go. I prayed repeatedly to stay with my parents in China. Finally, the day before I was to leave, I prayed that God would let me die before the next morning.

Obviously, God did not grant that request.

My sister Rosa and I boarded the *Nagasaki Maru,* and as the ship sailed down the Huangpu River . . .

I watched my parents slowly fade from sight.

VIRGINIA, ROSA, RUTH, AND VIRGINIA ON THE SHIP TO THE PYENG YANG FOREIGN SCHOOL.

The future is blank without a view.
That which I wanted most, You have denied;
I cannot understand (and I have tried);
There's nothing I can do but wait on You.

I spent most of my high school years in Korea. I didn't realize then that this initial separation from my parents would serve as my "spiritual boot camp" for the years that lay ahead.

Spare not the pain
    though the way I take
be lonely and dark,
    though the whole soul ache,
for the flesh must die
    though the heart may break.
Spare not the pain, oh,
    spare not the pain.

BACKGROUND: FACULTY, STAFF, AND STUDENTS AT THE PYENG YANG FOREIGN SCHOOL IN WHAT IS NORTH KOREA TODAY.

Boot Camp

GIGI GRAHAM TCHIVIDJIAN

The thirteen-year-old girl lay in the stifling heat of the old missionary home at Number Four Quinsan Gardens in the large port city of Shanghai, China, praying earnestly that she would die before morning.

Dawn broke over the gray city, and obviously God had not seen fit to answer her prayer.

It was September 2, 1933, and time for her to start high school. Her parents had chosen the Pyeng Yang Foreign School in what is today Pyongyang, North Korea.

Her older sister, Rosa, had been there the preceding year, and being a good adjuster, she enjoyed it thoroughly.

But, Ruth was different. She was leaving all that she loved and all that was familiar: her home, her parents, her friends, and thirteen years of treasured memories.

Five missionary children boarded the *Nagasake Maru*, berthed in the Whangpoo River, and moved slowly through the muddy waters to where the even muddier waters of the mighty Yangtze River emptied into the East China Sea.

The journey took the better part of a week. Finally they arrived in Pyeng Yang. They were met, transported, and deposited at the school. Ruth found herself in front of the gray-brick girls' dormitory.

PYENG YANG FOREIGN SCHOOL.

The homesickness settled in unmercifully. The days she could somehow manage. It was the nights that became unbearable. Burying her head in her pillow, she tried not to disturb her sleeping roommates.

Night after night, week after week, she cried herself to sleep, silently, miserably.

A few weeks later, Ruth became sick and was sent to the infirmary for several days. She propped herself up on her pillows and spent the entire time reading the Psalms, all 150 of them. The tiny corner room in the infirmary building still holds warm memories for Ruth because of the strength she received from those timeless, timely passages.

How could she know that this was her training period . . . her boot camp. Preparation for her future.

RUTH (FAR RIGHT, MIDDLE) IN A HOSPITAL
COMPOUND CLASSROOM BEFORE TRAVELING TO KOREA.

NORTH-CHINA DAILY NEWS
MAGAZINE SUPPLEMENT

No. 37

GRATIS

SHANGHAI, OCTOBER 3, 1937

BY 1937, I HAD MY FUTURE SECURELY PLANNED. I would never marry. I would spend the rest of my life as a missionary in Tibet. But on July 7 of that year, the Japanese attacked Chinese troops at the Marco Polo Bridge near Beijing, beginning the occupation of northern China. And while my father prepared for war, my mother prepared me for college in the United States.

I argued that all I needed was a utilitarian knowledge of Tibetan and the Bible. I certainly didn't have to sail halfway around the world for that.

My parents simply smiled and put me on a boat to the United States.

I was not happy.

THE NORTH-CHINA DAILY NEWS, OCTOBER 1

An Air-Raid on Nanki

Spectators during the first Japanese raid on Nankin see one of the Japanese aeroplanes brought down in flames.

"Rock of Ages cleft for me,
let me hide myself in thee."

So helpless a thing my heart
    —and, oh, so small—
all overwhelmed, it looks to You for strength,
    nor looks in vain;
long it has struggled on, and now at length
    is crushed again.

Eager with expectation, rising
    but to fall,
wearily it longs for that great Rock
    "higher than I,"
where, with Your strength absorbing every shock,
    calm shall I lie.

Test me, O Lord, and give me strength
    to meet each test
unflinching, unafraid:
not striving nervously to do my best,
not self-assured, or careless as in
    jest,
but with Your aid.

Purge me, Lord, and give me grace to
    bear the heat
of cleansing flame:
not bitter at my lowly lot, but mete
to bear my share of suffering and keep
    sweet,
in Jesus' Name.

As a seventeen-year-old aboard the USS *McKinley*, halfway across the Pacific Ocean, I found myself making up a list.

If *I marry*:

He must be so tall when he is on his knees, as one has said, he reaches all the way to Heaven.

His shoulders must be broad enough to bear the burden of a family.

His lips must be strong enough to smile,

firm enough to say no,

and tender enough to kiss.

His love must be so deep that it takes its stand in

Christ and so wide that it takes in the whole world.

He must be big enough to be gentle

and great enough to be thoughtful.

His arms must be strong enough to carry a little child.

A rather odd list for a "confirmed spinster."

College and Early Marriage

ROSA AND RUTH WITH THEIR FATHER IN
MONTREAT, NORTH CAROLINA SHORTLY
AFTER RUTH'S MARRIAGE.

With quiet eyes aglow,
I'll understand that he's the man
I prayed for long ago.

RUTH BELL GRAHAM

I ARRIVED ON THE WHEATON COLLEGE CAMPUS dressed in hand-me-downs and size 7 saddle shoes. And being a freshman, promptly placed upon my head was an orange-and-green "dink."

After one week of college I wrote . . .

Teach me contentment, Lord, whate'er my lot,
keeping my eyes on You in trust,
knowing Your love is true, Your way is just.

Teach discontentment, Lord, with what I am;
daily striving, growing daily nearer,
finding You are daily closer, dearer.

Contented, Lord, yet discontented make me,
both together working, blending
all in Your own glory ending.

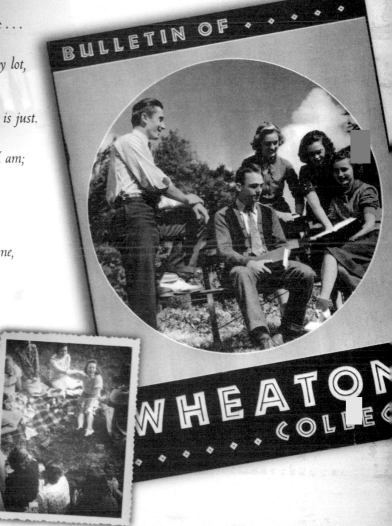

I FOUND MY TYPICAL DAILY SCHEDULE IN AN OLD NOTEBOOK:

3 a.m. Devotions

4–7 a.m. Study Greek

7 a.m. Get dressed

8 a.m. Greek

9 Lit

10 Chapel . . . Mandatory

1: 10:30 Study history

11:30 History

NOON.

2, 3, 4: Lunch!

Whew.

12:30 p.m. Archery

1:30 Bible Class

3:30 Tower picture

4:30 Art lab

5:30 Supper

6:30–8:30 Special Feature

8:30 (*yawning*) Study Greek

9:30–10:30 House Prayer Meeting

11 p.m.

(*Snores*)

Shhhhhh.

THEN WITH LESS THAN ONE MONTH OF COLLEGE under my belt, I was almost kicked out.

You see, a number of upperclassmen had been vying for my attention. There were dinners and ice shows in Chicago!

On two occasions my escorts chose to ignore the 10:30 curfew. They considered it bothersome. It was after midnight when I was deposited in front of Williston Hall.

My dorm room was the last one on the west end, just close enough to the ground to slip behind the boxwoods and, with a boost up, crawl over the sill.

On my second Friday night of crime, I was intercepted by the dorm mother. "Where have you been and how did you get in?"

"I've been on a date and I climbed through the window."

"I see. You blatantly chose to ignore the rules outlined in your student handbook."

The handbook was a compilation of regulations outlining dozens of petty sins. I had thought the original Big Ten enough. See, I'd come from a world of air raids, bandits, and Japanese bombers, so this new threat of curfew did not impress me. First thing Monday morning I reported to the dean of students.

"You have disgraced the school. You have disgraced your parents. You have disgraced yourself. You can choose between expulsion or an indefinite campusing."

I chose to be campused, while my dates, who were responsible for returning me to campus after curfew, went unpunished.

Sound familiar?

I was not allowed to go out on dates.

I was not allowed to leave school grounds.

I was not allowed a defense.

"The Lord shall fight for you, and you shall hold your peace."

I found I had plenty of time to write.

"What a friend we have in Jesus all our sin and griefs to bear"...

Pray
   when all your soul
   on tiptoe stands
   in wistful eagerness
   to talk with God;
   put out your hands,
   God bends to hear;
   it would be sin
   not to draw near.

Pray
   when gray inertia
   creeps through your soul,
   as through a man
   who fights the cold,
   then growing languid
   slumbereth,
   and slumbering
   knows not
   it is death.

Pray
   when swamped
   with sin and shame
   and nowhere else
   to pin the blame
   but your own will
   and waywardness;
   God knows you,
   loves you nonetheless.

So . . . pray.

Dear God,

let me soar in the face of the wind;

up—

up—

like the lark,

so poised and so sure,

through the cold

on the storm

with wings to endure.

Let the silver rain wash

all the dust from my wings,

let me soar

as he soars,

let me sing

as he sings

let it lift me

all joyous

and carefree

and swift,

let it buffet

and drive me

but, God,

Let it lift!

The Coat

GIGI GRAHAM TCHIVIDJIAN

One semester, when Mother was at Wheaton College, she and her friend Elizabeth Walker decided that they would give up the privilege of eating in the "upper dining hall," which was much more pleasant, and move to the "lower dining hall," which was in the basement of Williston Hall, one of the girls' dormitories, in order to give the extra money to a student whom they thought was in real need.

Later, Mother saw this student whom they were helping anonymously wearing a coat that Mother could never have afforded.

She was surprised and indignant. She was sacrificing for this student, and this student seemed better off than she was.

But then, she heard a still, quiet voice asking her, *Are you doing this for her or for Me?*

Mother had to admit that she and her friend were doing this because they both loved Him.

That is all I wanted to hear, He said.

It was all Mother needed to know. From then on, the other student could have worn mink, and it wouldn't have made any difference to Mother.

Many years later, Mother was in Amsterdam at the Congress of Itinerant Evangelists, a conference that brought thousands of evangelists from around

the world together in order to teach and encourage them. Most of these came from Third World countries.

On one of the last days of the conference, Mother was helping in the clothing room. An African man came in looking for a dress for his wife. The clothing room had been pretty well picked over by this time, and there was not much left. After spending some time looking, this man could not find anything. Quickly, Mother went behind the curtain, took off her own dress, and, putting on whatever she could find to cover herself, gave it to this man to take home to his wife in Africa.

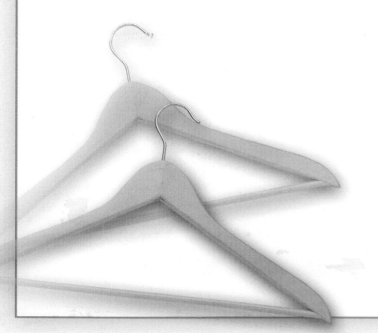

Jesus said, "When you have done it unto one of the least of these, you do it for Me."

By the spring of my freshman year, the Wheaton faculty realized that my "infractions" were committed out of ignorance, not wickedness. They "lifted" my sentence. My journals attest to the fresh outlook I had on everything.

Tell me
how
the setting sun,
briefly glimpsed
through wet
black clouds,
can
to molten gold
with ease,
kindle
sodden limbs
of trees.

I mean everything.

RUTH WITH HAROLD LINDSELL,
LATER TO BECOME AN AUTHOR,
THEOLOGIAN, AND EDITOR OF
CHRISTIANITY TODAY.

Dear God, I prayed,
(as we're inclined to do).
I do not need a handsome man
but let him be like You;
I do not need one big and strong
nor yet so very tall,
nor need he be some genius,
or wealthy, Lord, at all;
but let his head be high, dear God,
and let his eye be clear,
his shoulders straight, whate'er his state,
whate'er his earthly sphere;
and let his face have character,
a ruggedness of soul

Dear God, I prayed, all unafraid
(as we're inclined to do),
I do not need a handsome man
but let him be like You;
I do not need one big and strong
nor yet so very tall,
nor need he be some genius,
or wealthy, Lord, at all;
but let his head be high, dear God,
and let his eye be clear,
his shoulders straight, whate'er his state,
whate'er his earthly sphere;
and let his face have character,
a ruggedness of soul,
and let his whole life show, dear God,
a singleness of goal;
then when he comes
(as he will come)
with quiet eyes aglow,
I'll understand that he's the man
I prayed for long ago.

Lay them quietly at His feet
    one by one:
each desire, however sweet,
    just begun;
dreams still hazy, growing bright;
hope just poised, winged for flight;
all your longing each delight—
    every one.
At His feet and leave them there,
    never fear;
every heartache, crushing care—
    trembling tear;
you will find Him always true,
men may fail you, friends be few,
He will prove Himself to you
    far more dear.

Bastards?

GIGI GRAHAM TCHIVIDJIAN

W hat did you have for Thanksgiving dinner in China?" asked Mother's dinner companion, Harold Lindsell, one Thanksgiving at Wheaton College. "Turkey?"

"No," Mother replied. "We ate bastards."

Looking a bit shocked, he exclaimed, "I doubt that!"

Mother became a bit incensed.

"Yes," she insisted. "We did, too. We ate them every Thanksgiving. They were quite good."

Looking at her a bit strangely, he said, "I don't think so."

Upset by his attitude, she replied indignantly, "Well, I ought to know. I've eaten plenty of them!"

Whereupon he quickly changed the subject.

Later, when she recounted this episode to her older sister, Rosa, she burst out laughing.

"What is so funny?" Mother asked.

"You nut!" Rosa exclaimed. "They were not *bastards*, but *bustards*—wild geese called bustards."

IT WAS EARLY FALL IN 1940 WHEN WILLIAM FRANKLIN GRAHAM arrived on campus via the Wheaton College Student Trucking Service, run by Johnny Streater.

Billy Frank was a twenty-one-year-old North Carolinian, already an ordained Baptist minister, with clear blue eyes, standing six-foot-two.

It was so very good of God
to let my dreams come true,
to note a young girl's cherished hopes,
then lead her right to you;
so good of Him to take such care
in little, detailed parts
(He knows how much details mean
to young and wishful hearts);
so good of Him to let you be
tall and slender, too,
with waving hair more blond than brown
and eyes of steel blue.

On our first date we attended the school's presentation of the Messiah. "HALLELUJAH." I agonized over which of my two homemade dresses to wear.

BACKGROUND: RUTH AND BILLY OUTSIDE THE CHURCH AT WESTERN SPRINGS, ILLINOIS, BILLY'S FIRST FULL-TIME PASTORATE.

Your eyes look down at me
so thoughtfully . . .
What do they see?
The plainness of me—
plainly built,
not small,
nor calmly poised,
nor quaint,
and, worst of all,
a nose upturned
and hands that I have known
for years to be
too long,
too overgrown;

plain hazel eyes,
a face too pale, not fair,
a mouth too large
and ordinary hair?
and all of me
tucked in
this homemade dress;
oh, if you look at me
so thoughtfully,
will you love me
the less?

After that first date, I knelt beside my bed and prayed, "God, if You let me serve You with that man, I'd consider it the greatest privilege of my life."

BILLY FRANK BECAME THE MOST POPULAR SUBJECT in my journals, my poetry, and my letters. But our relationship went nowhere.

I began 1941 by flunking Greek and ancient history. Finally . . .

February 7. He invited me to go to church to hear him preach.

I was surprised. He spoke with such authority . . . and, at the same time, humility. The star, seen and admired from afar, became a human, personal thing—within reach.

We drove back to campus in his 1937 green Plymouth. I watched his profile as he guided us through the Chicago traffic and marked the glint in his eyes where the streetlights flashed past.

I had felt the firmness of his hand beneath my arm as he guided me through the crowd at the church. I was impressed by his unaffected thoughtfulness . . .

As he walked me to the door, he said, "There's something I'd like you to make a matter of prayer. I have been taking you out because I am more than interested in you and have been since the day Johnny Streater introduced us last fall. But I know you have been called to the mission field, and I'm not definite."

SOMETHING BIG WAS HAPPENING.

*I looked into your face and knew
that you were true;
those clear deep eyes awoke in me
a trust in you.*

*I'd dreamt of shoulders broad and straight,
one built to lead;
I met you once and knew that you
were all I need.*

I was so naive wasn't I?

*You did not have to say a word
to make me feel
that will, completely in control,
was made of steel.*

*I'd dreamt of dashing love and bold,
life wild with zest;
but when with you my heart was stilled
to perfect rest.*

*And how? I could not understand,
it seemed so odd:
till on my heart it quietly dawned
—love is of God!*

I WROTE TO MY PARENTS:

"Despite Bill's fearlessness and sometimes sternness, he is just as thoughtful and gentle as one would want a man to be. Maybe it's the South in him. . . . Sounds like I'm in love, doesn't it? Don't get worried. I'm not."

Another date.

You held my hand
and I,
feeling a strange,
sweet thrill,
gave to my heart
a sharp rebuke,
and told it
to be still.

You held me close
and I
gasped, "Oh, no!"
until
I felt my heart within me rise
and tell me
to be still.

BILLY GRAHAM ON RUTH'S
BOYFRIENDS IN COLLEGE

Ruth had a lot of boyfriends.
In college her sister kept a count
of the different men that she dated.
She had a list of fifty-two.
I don't think I dated more than two at college.

"I haven't tried to win you, Ruth. I haven't asked you to fall in love with me. I haven't sent you candy and flowers and lovely gifts. I have asked the Lord, if you are the one, to win you for me. If not, to keep you from falling in love with me."

I started dating other men.

"Either you date just me or you can date everybody but me."

"I think being an old-maid missionary is the highest calling there is."

"Woman was created to be a wife and a mother."

"God has many exceptions, and I believe I'm one of them."

FROM RUTH'S COLLEGE
JOURNAL: ON BILLY

You know—funny how the little things pop up in the memory. His way of going about things, his self-control . . . the way he put both hands on the wheel and squared his shoulders when we began, the strength and keenness of his profile when the streetlight fell thru the snow sifting on the windshield and lit up his face. I wasn't watching him directly, but one sees a lot out of the corner of one's eye. Oh, I shouldn't be writing all this. You'll think me a romantic nitwit.

Asking Ruth for a Date

BILLY GRAHAM

While working my way through school I worked on a furniture truck. The man who ran the truck, Johnny Streater, had been in the military in the Far East before World War II. He kept telling me about this girl who was the most beautiful girl he had ever met. And he said she got up every morning at 4 A.M. to pray. I thought, *What a wonderful person she must be.* But I had already been in love once (down in Florida where I went to a Bible school) and didn't want to go through it again because it was painful.

One day I saw a girl walk across the campus and I thought, *She is gorgeous.* At the time I didn't know this was the girl Johnny talked about.

Later, I was in my work clothes and we had just pulled up in front of the women's dorm hauling furniture and had just gotten off the furniture truck. That was where Johnny introduced me to Ruth.

I felt embarrassed and ill at ease because I'd already built her up so much in my mind. My friends around me said, "Ask her for a date." But I couldn't get the courage to do it because I knew she was popular with other boys.

Finally, I saw her in study hall and one of my friends said, "Go over and ask her." I finally got up enough nerve to sit down beside her and I said, "They're going to perform *The Messiah* on Sunday afternoon just before Christmas. Could I take you to *The Messiah?*"

She sort of turned, nodded her head, and said, "Yes," in a low voice (because we were in the library). So I took her, and on the way back to her dorm in the snow I tried to hold her hand and she pulled it away. I'll never forget that.

How rejected I felt. I said to myself, "Well, I failed with this one anyway."

But a few days later we did get together and have another date.

I FELT AS IF I WERE BEATING MY FIST against a wall. I was afraid I was losing myself. I didn't

know what the Lord would have me do . . .

Insomnia

Tossing

Turning

Thinking

Tossing

Turning

Tears

Misery.

I shall leave it here

beneath this star

tonight;

no one will see me

leave it

with only a star

for light;

no one will know

I stood here,

hoarding a heaviness,   *striving for liberty:*

clutching tightly   *I'll love it,*

in eager hands   *and leave it,*

something of loveliness;   *and then forget;*

something   *and forgetting—*

that struggled against me   *I shall be free!*

The Blur

GIGI GRAHAM TCHIVIDJIAN

All she saw was a blur.

Mother was going up the stairs, and he was going down.

Boy, that young man is in a hurry, she thought and she went on.

Mother and Daddy were both students at Wheaton College in Illinois. Sunday mornings, those students who were involved in gospel team assignments had a prayer meeting. The next Sunday, Mother heard a new voice pray. It was strong, clear, urgent.

There is a man who knows to whom he is speaking, she thought.

She had heard about this new student from a Bible college in Florida. It was told that he was a gifted preacher—a young man on whose shoulder God's hand seemed to rest.

One day a friend introduced them and not long after that, Daddy asked Mother for their first date—a Sunday afternoon presentation of *The Messiah.*

Mother has said that, although she didn't have much of a chance to get to know him that night, she knew that he was the one.

She prayed, "Lord if You will let me spend the rest of my life with that man, I will count it the greatest privilege possible."

But . . .

There was Tibet.

Mother had always wanted to go to Tibet as a missionary. She tried to gently, persistently persuade Daddy that perhaps he, too, should go to Tibet as a missionary.

After several weeks of this, Daddy finally asked her, "Do you believe that God brought us together?"

"Of course I do," she quickly replied.

"Then," Daddy answered gently but firmly, "God will lead me and you will do the following."

She has been following ever since.

Recently, Daddy added a little of his side to this story.

"She wanted me to agree that I would go to Tibet as a missionary. And I told her that I didn't feel I was called to do that. But she felt she had to marry someone who was willing to go to Tibet, so I asked for the ring back. But she wouldn't take it off, and she wouldn't let me take it off. So she changed her mind right there."

"You sent for me, Ruth."

"I think I know now, Bill."

"When did you decide?"

"I don't know . . . but I thought it only fair, Bill, to tell you . . ."

"Yes?"

"That I love you."

Only the pounding of his heart told me he had not known what to expect.

I recall the way the stars looked . . . distant and bright . . . the way the night wind blew through his hair . . . the look in his eye.

He reached for my hand. Smiling, he gathered me to him a moment. "I would like to kiss you . . . but I think I should wait."

My love has been yours . . .
since on that day
when first we met—
I will never quite forget
how you just paused
and smiled a bit,
then calmly helped yourself to it.

When Bill was young, he wanted to play professional baseball, and I wanted to go to Tibet. In truth, neither of us had any business doing either . . .

MEANWHILE, I BECAME INCREASINGLY ANXIOUS for my parents, still in China. It took two months for letters to arrive.

In 1941, my mother became seriously ill. In May, she and my father sailed to the United States. In August, the Japanese took captive the remaining Quinjiang missionaries.

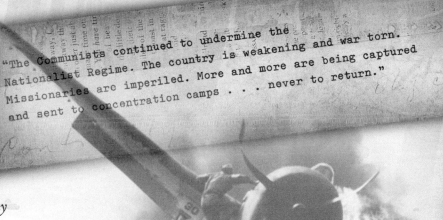

"The Communists continued to undermine the Nationalist Regime. The country is weakening and war torn. Missionaries are imperiled. More and more are being captured and sent to concentration camps . . . never to return."

It won't be long—
the sun is slowly slipping out of sight;
lengthening shadows deepen into dusk;
still winds whisper;
all is quiet:
it won't be long
—till night.

It won't be long—
the tired eyes close,
her strength is nearly gone;
frail hands that ministered to many
lie quiet, still;
Light from another world!
Look up, bereaved!
It won't be long
—till Dawn!

IN SEPTEMBER—"THE RING." It was purchased with every penny of the sixty-five-dollar love offering Billy had received from Sharon Presbyterian Church.

God,
let me be all he ever dreamed
of loveliness and laughter.
Veil his eyes a bit
because
there are so many little flaws;
somehow, God,
please let him see
only the bride I long to be,
remembering ever after—
I was all he ever dreamed
of loveliness and laughter.

Those sentiments were rather youthful . . . and short-lived.

FROM RUTH'S COLLEGE JOURNAL:
PREDICTION ON MARRYING BILLY

If I marry Bill I must marry him with my eyes open. He will be increasingly burdened for lost souls and increasingly active in the Lord's work. After the joy and satisfaction of knowing that I am his by rights—and his forever, I will slip into the background. . . . In short, be a lost life. Lost in Bill's.

"I will not become a Baptist. I have always been and will always remain in the Presbyterian Church!"

"I'd like you to raise a family."

"I still think I should be a missionary."

"Listen, do you or do you not think the Lord brought us together?"

"Yes."

"Then I'll do the leading and you'll do the following."

I almost slapped the ring back into his hand—

Train our love . . .
Discipline it, too . . .
Deepen it
throughout the years,
age and mellow it
until, time that finds us
old without,
within,
will find us
lovers still.

I've been following ever since.

FRIDAY, AUGUST 13, 1943
The Montreat Presbyterian Church . . .

"With this ring I thee wed . . ."
your strong, familiar voice
fell like a benediction
on my heart, that dusk;
tall candles flickered gently,
our age-old vows were said,
and I could hear
someone begin to sing
an old, old song,
timeworn and lovely,
timeworn and dear.
And in that dusk
were old, old friends—
and you,
an old friend, too
(and dearer than them all).
Only my ring seemed new—
its plain gold surface
warm and bright
and strange to me
that candlelight . . .
unworn—unmarred.
Could it be that wedding rings
like other things,
are lovelier when scarred?

RUTH GRAHAM ON MARRIAGE

"If two people agree on everything . . .
one of them is unnecessary."

Never let it end, God,
never—please—
all this growing loveliness,
all of these
brief moments of
fresh pleasure—
never let it end,
Let us always
be a little breathless
at love's beauty;
never let us pause to reason
from a sense of duty;
never let us
stop to measure
just how much to give;
never let us
stoop to weigh love;
let us live—
and live!

Please God,
let our hearts kneel always,
Love their only Master,
knowing the warm impulsiveness
of shattered alabaster:
I know You can see things
the way a new bride sees,
so
never let it end, God,
never—please.

WE HAD SAVED SEVENTY-FIVE DOLLARS for the honeymoon in Blowing Rock. Needless to say, it was a short one.

Off we drove to Hinsdale, Illinois, where Billy had taken a pastorate at the Western Springs Baptist Church.

I was not altogether in favor of this. I believed Billy's call was to evangelism and not to the pastorate. He was receiving invitations to preach throughout the Midwest, which was a strain on his home church duties, and rarely was it financially possible for me to go with him.

SO THE SEPARATIONS BEGAN.

"Beneath the cross of Jesus" . . .

When
in the morning
I make our bed,
pulling his sheets
and covers tight,
I know the tears
I shouldn't shed
will fall unbidden
as the rain;
and I would kneel,
praying again
words I mean
but cannot feel.

"Lord,
not my will
but Thine
be done."
The doubts dissolving
one by one . . .

For I realize
as I pray,
that's why it happened
. . . and this way.

I FOUND GOD WAS CONTINUALLY OPENING my heart to more . . . I wrote this after the first funeral Billy conducted.

"I'm Daniel Creasman's mother.
I brung these clothes
so's you
could dress him up real natural-like—
no . . .
navy wouldn't do.
He liked this little playsuit—
it's sorta faded now—
that tore place he
he got tryin' to help his daddy plow.
No . . .
if he dressed real smart-like—
and all that fancy trim—
the last we'd see of Danny,
it wouldn't seem
like him.
But . . .
comb his hair . . . real special
(if 'twouldn't seem
too odd) . . .
I'll brush it so
come Sunday when he goes
to the house of God."

That afternoon
I saw him—
so still, so tanned he lay—
with the faded blue suit on him,
like he'd just come in from play . . .
but his hair was brushed
"real special" . . .
and it didn't seem one bit odd, for . . .
he was just a small boy,
done with play
gone home to the house of God.

ONE DAY A GROUP OF YOUNG PREACHERS we knew had gathered—I can't remember what for—and were talking about an Asian student—how much he had sacrificed leaving a wife and six children at home while he studied for his degree in America.

I, however, saw the sacrifice from a different perspective.

Bless him,
Lord,
in leaving
all
for You—
bereft;
bless him,
Lord,
but pity
the left.

Bless the sacrificial,
yielding
the dearly priced;
bless him,
Lord,
but pity
the sacrificed.

Bless each valiant warrior
wherever he may roam;
bless him, Lord;
but pity
those back home.

To keep me company, I used to sleep with Bill's tweed jacket when he was away.

I kept my mind occupied with Bible study and reading. When Billy hosted *Songs in the Night*—a program of singing and preaching on the radio—I'd pass him notes of suggestions. And quotations from the biographies, histories, and novels I'd been reading.

And all during World War II, I continued to write.

The field that night
was a sea of mud,
the wet sky seared with flame;
each bursting shell,
like a blast from hell,
lit the spot
where a soldier fell.

There in the blackness,
lying low,
weakly
he spoke His name.

For
where the lust of man
runs loose
through stench and smoke
of hate white-hot,
where lives
and souls
are cheaply priced,

there walks the Christ.
The sin scarred
brush
His white, white robes;
the wounded
touch His feet;
the dying whisper
His name in prayer,
wondering sweetly
to find Him there,
where hell
and the sinner meet.

He too of His grace . . .
His infinite grace . . . .
And soldiers wondered
to find a trace
of tears
in the grime
on a dead man's face.

"The going
must've been tough,"
they said,
not knowing,
that death,
for a man
forgiven by God,
is easy going.

IN THE MID-1940S, BILLY HAD RESIGNED from the pastorate, applied for an army chaplaincy, and then become a full-time evangelist for a new organization, Youth for Christ. We moved to Montreat, North Carolina, to be near my parents. But Bill's preaching schedule was busier than ever, and our separations became more frequent.

MONTREAT CHURCH,
NORTH CAROLINA.

In 1950, the Billy Graham Evangelistic Association was born. Separation now seemed to be the rule and not the exception.

We live in a time
secure;
beloved and loving,
sure
it cannot last
for long
then—
the good-byes come
again—again—
like a small death,
the closing of a door.
One learns to live
with pain.
One looks ahead,
not back—
never back,
only before.
And joy will come again—
warm and secure,
if only for the now,
laughing,
we endure.

The original Billy Graham Evangelistic Team. From left to right: George Beverly Shea, Grady Wilson, Billy Graham, Tedd Smith, and Cliff Barrows.

Little Piney Cove

Piney Cove

I returned home
a little while later realizing
that I, too, had been refreshed in
their presence just watching and
listening to "plenty of nothin'."

GIGI GRAHAM TCHIVIDJIAN

1954!

We'd been offered a good deal on a hundred-and-fifty-acre cove located between two hogbacks, two ridges, on one of the Seven Sisters.

The price: forty-three hundred dollars.

Billy surveyed the property with some skepticism.

My blood raced at the potential, but Billy had to leave for the West Coast.

"I leave it up to you to decide."

I borrowed the money from the bank and bought the cove. Billy came home and said, "You what?!"

But this was to become our home . . . the place to return to . . . the place of sustenance and love.

A Charming Cove

RUTH BELL GRAHAM

Billy, there's a little cove I'd like to show you," Mike Wiley said to Bill one day. "It belongs to a couple of mountain families, but I think you could buy it reasonably."

"Let's go," Bill said. "We'll take my car."

"Won't make it," Mike objected. "Road's too narrow. Get in my Jeep."

That's how we first saw it. The road was incredibly narrow, winding, and steep. Old man Solomon Morris had originally built it, using first a mule and a plow, followed by a mule and a drag pan. Eventually, a mule could make it up with a wagon. And a Jeep could make it. The rhododendron bushes crowded in on both sides.

After what seemed a long time, we passed a modest shack on our left, covered with tarpaper, windows, and doors filled with staring, unsmiling faces. The right side of the narrow road dropped almost vertically to the tiny streambed below. Evidence of a harvested corn crop in this unlikely spot gave a clue as to how the family supplemented its meager income.

As we rounded the next curve, we had to slow down to ford the same streamlet that passed through a tiny valley on our left, crossed the dirt road, and dropped on down the mountain. Around the next bend beneath a cluster of large, freshly topped white pines on the outcropping of the hogback above and a small pole cabin to our right, we reached the end of the road.

Those two mountain families and two old bachelors had scraped a living off these acres mainly by harvesting the larger trees for lumber, so that all that remained were the culled ones.

The number of gallon jars confirmed our idea of how else they supplemented the harvesting of trees. I have real sympathy for mountain families living out cold winters in unheated cabins: They might just need some antifreeze.

Not having garbage collection, whenever they finished with something, they simply pitched it down the mountain. It was all pretty sorry looking, but it was a generous chunk of land and the price was reasonable—somewhere between twelve and fourteen dollars an acre.

Finally Bill said, "I'll leave it up to you, Ruth. While I'm in California, you decide." It was isolated, it was loaded with possibilities, and I loved it. So while he was in California, I borrowed the money from the bank and bought it.

When Bill returned, I told him.

"You what?" he exclaimed.

"What wondrous love is this oh,
my soul, oh, my soul,
what wondrous love is this, oh, my soul" . . .

The candle flames
of poplars,
in the little coves
burn low;
the woods, leaf-carpeted
are warm
with Autumn's afterglow.
There's frost
upon the air tonight,
a hint of coming cold;
still, the warmth
of Summer lingers
in the crimson
and the gold.

Give me a cove
——a little cove——
when Fall comes
amblin' round:
hint of frost
upon the air,
sunlight
on the ground;

a little cove
with poplars——
calm
and
straight
and
tall;
to burn like candle flames
against
the sullen gray
of Fall.

P. S.
We bought this cove
when coves were cheap,
flatland scarce,
mountains steep.
Not once
were we ever told
in Autumn
poplars
turn to gold.

Oh, it was cheap
(beyond belief)
but Autumn makes me feel
a thief!

If I could have each day
one hour of sun,
glorious,
healing,
hot,
like now—
then let Winter come!
Not
mild and brief,
but
wild, without relief;
let the storms rage,
let the winds blow,
the freezing rains
lashing my windowpanes;
then let it snow!
long
and
deep
and cold.
I would not mind at all:
it would be fun . . .
if I could have
each day
my hour of sun.

Winter speaks
to the surfeited heart,
weary of heat
and weeds
and leaves,
longing to breathe
cold, bracing air,
explore the hillsides
swept and bare;
to revel in each bush,
each tree,
stripped to stark
simplicity;
original etchings
everywhere—
and You,
Who etched them,
with me there.

I am a primitive.
I love
primordial silences
that reign
unbroken over ridge
and plain,
unspoiled by
civilization's roar.
I love the lonesome sound
of wind,
the final crashing
of a tree,
the wash of waves
upon the shore,
wind, thunder, and
the pouring rain
are symphonies to me.

It was also the perfect place to raise a family.

A Quiet Midsummer's Eve

GIGI GRAHAM TCHIVIDJIAN

The hot August afternoon turned into a soft, cool evening. After an early supper, I decided to drive up to Daddy and Mother's for a visit.

I found the two of them sitting quietly on the front porch, as is often their habit on a summer's evening. We watched the dogs playing and the birds pecking the ground around the feeder for any missed or dropped seeds. We watched as dusk slowly turned to dark and the little lights flickered on in the valley below, waiting to see which of us would spot the first lightning bug and hear the first katydid of the evening.

Sitting there with these two very special people in the sunset of their lives brought back so many memories.

I couldn't help but remember something Mother wrote about one such evening many years ago.

Rocking quietly on this same porch watching the evening creep slowly up the ridges, she heard the screen door slam. My then six-year-old brother settled in beside her and said, "Shhh. Be quiet, Mom. Don't make any noise . . . and you will hear plenty of nuffin."

With that he bounded up as quickly as he had arrived, disappearing back inside and slamming the screen door behind him.

Mother sat and thought to herself, *I like plenty of nothin'.*

Later she wrote, "It's the noise of civilization that disturbs and grates on the nerves. Nature's noises refresh and relax me . . . the rustle of the wind in the tops of the trees or the roar of it across the ridge behind the house. The chirping of a cricket or the orchestration of katydids from midsummer until frost. The full moon rising, huge and silent, the unexpected stillness. . . . On such evenings alone or with Bill when he is home, we sit quietly talking or just listening to plenty of nothin'."

I returned home a little while later realizing that I, too, had been refreshed in their presence just watching and listening to "plenty of nothin'."

Family

*My mother is
a very unpredictable woman,
and I'm sure I get plenty
of my spunk from her.*

FRANKLIN GRAHAM

Five I have:

Three daughters, right in a row.
Gigi
Anne
and Bunny.
Because she looked like a rabbit.
And two sons.
Franklin
and Ned.

each separate,
distinct,
a soul
bound for eternity:
and I
—blind leader of the blind—
groping and fumbling,
casual and concerned,
by turns . . .
undisciplined, I seek
by order and command
to discipline and shape;
(I who need Thy discipline
to shape my own disordered soul).
O Thou
Who seest the heart's

true, deep desire,
each shortcoming and
each sad mistake,
supplement
and
overrule,
nor let our children be
the victims of our own
unlikeness unto Thee.

ANNE GRAHAM LOTZ ON
RUTH BELL GRAHAM

My mother . . . made God's Word
"more to be desired than gold" by her
own example, and her loving encourage-
ment, sensitive insights, and unwavering
support have kept me going during dark
moments of weary discouragement.

Gigi—never was there a little girl who
tried so hard to be good,
but was so bad at it.

Carefree, she ran into the park to play,
her face uplifted to the sun;
that day . . .
aware of brewing storms
that etched the sky,
clutched at a fear
and nursed it.
Then I
saw her hand
outstretched
like a small child;
and while I watched,
Another Hand
reached down and clasped it.

I heard the distant thunder
with a smile.

Am I Going to Heaven?

GIGI GRAHAM TCHIVIDJIAN

In the mid 1950s as Daddy became better known, the tourists descended on our small home by the bus load. It soon became evident that they would have to do something to ensure our family a certain amount of privacy. My parents decided that we would have to move after Mother discovered tourists peeping in her bedroom window.

A charming cove was offered to them for thirteen dollars an acre. When Daddy left for his next trip he told Mother to make the final decision. She promptly went to the bank and borrowed the money to purchase Little Piney Cove, which has proved again and again such a blessing. Mother's first project was to transform one of the small pole cabins into a weekend hideaway.

It was a one-room cabin with a loft. The kitchen consisted of a rock fireplace and a grill outside. Water was piped in from a spring to a wooden tub at the side door, and the bathroom was an outhouse down a narrow dark path some 100 feet from the cabin. Mother furnished it with comfortable, simple, old secondhand pieces. A big, high old double bed was placed behind a curtain at one end and mattresses were laid in the loft for us children.

Mother promised to take me, Anne, and Bunny to the cabin to spend the night. One day when we arrived home from school, Mother piled us into the Jeep and soon we were bouncing along the old dirt road that climbed steeply upward toward the cabin.

After a supper of hot dogs and hot chocolate prepared over the open fire, we sat on the porch, reading and talking until dark. Suddenly I asked a question that had been troubling me all afternoon.

"Mama, if I die, will I go to heaven?" I had good reason to ask, for that very afternoon, for the umpteenth time, I had been punished for teasing my younger sisters unmercifully.

"You tell me," Mama replied.

"I don't know," I answered.

"Do you want me to tell you how you can know?"

"I don't think you can know for sure," I replied.

"Oh, yes, you can," said Mama.

"How?" I asked skeptically.

"First," she explained, "you know that you are a sinner, don't you?"

"Of course!" I quickly answered. I never seemed to have any doubt about that since I was always getting into trouble.

"Then you confess your sins to the Lord," Mama explained.

"I've done that," I continued. "After I got so mad this afternoon, I told Him I was sorry three times—just in case He didn't hear me the first time."

"He heard you the first time," Mama replied. "You are a child of God because you asked Jesus into your heart. Do you remember being born into God's family when you were only four?"

"No." I shook my head. "I don't remember it. I only know what you've told me. And I'm still not sure I'm going to heaven."

"Gigi, just because you can't remember the day doesn't make it any less real." Mama's voice became gentle but firm. "Would you call God a liar?"

"Of course not!" I protested.

"But that's just what you're doing," she insisted. "He tells us that if we confess, He will forgive. You have confessed and you believe—yet you don't think God will keep His promise? That's the same as calling Him a liar." Mama paused a moment for me to reflect on her words. "Don't you recall John 3:16?" asked Mother. "Recite it for me."

I repeated the familiar, much-loved verse: "'For God so loved the world, that he gave his only begotten Son, that whosoever believeth in him should not perish, but have everlasting life'" (KJV).

Then Mama held up a piece of paper and said, "Whoever wants it can have it."

I quickly snatched it from her fingers.

"What makes you think I said you?" Mama asked.

"You said, 'whoever,'" I replied.

"Exactly," answered Mother.

My little face slowly lit up. Then we knelt by the bed and prayed for assurance of my salvation.

"Mama," I said breathlessly as we rose to our feet, "I feel like a new person."

The next day, this "new person" scampered down Assembly Drive to the Montreat gate and uprooted a dozen water lilies that had just been planted in time for the arrival of the season's first tourists and conferees. Mama escorted me to the town manager's office with the evidence wilting in my tight little fist, my face pale as I worried aloud that I was going to be thrown into jail. (Mama said nothing to dispel the fear.)

I confessed and apologized. With so much practice, I was a good little "repenter."

That night as Mama tucked me into bed, I asked plaintively, "Have I been good enough today to go to heaven?"

"Now, how much," Mama wrote in her diary that night, "should I impress on Gigi the doctrine of salvation by grace when, really, for a child of her disposition, one could be tempted to think that salvation by works would be more effective?"

Anne and Bunny.

You see, Anne was a remarkably gentle and loving child . . . usually.

(Screams)

However, one day

(Screams)

I ran to the kitchen to find Bunny, age three, holding her hand over her cheek and keeping a very close eye on Anne, age five.

"What on earth is the matter?"

"It's all right, Mommy. I'm teaching Bunny about the Bible. I'm slapping her on one cheek and teaching her to turn the other one so I can slap it, too."

For all these smallnesses
I thank You, Lord:

small children
and small needs;
small meals to cook,
small talk to heed,
and a small book
from which to read
small stories;
small hurts to heal,
small disappointments, too,
as real
as ours;
small glories
to discover
in bugs,
pebbles,
flowers.

When day is through
my mind is small,
my strength is gone;
and as I gather
each dear one
I pray, "Bless each
for Jesus' sake—
such angels sleeping, imps awake!"

What wears me out
are little things:
angels minus
shining wings.
Forgive me, Lord,
if I have whined—
it takes so much

to keep them shined;
yet each small rub
has its reward,
for they have blessed me.

Thank You,
Lord.

Franklin Graham on Ruth Bell Graham

Like many boys living in a family populated with older girls, I chose to establish my place in the family by pestering my sisters to death. As I grew older, a good day for me was to have all three of them either crying or screaming at once, and me still laughing. But, of course, that got me in trouble.

A treat for us was to go into the "big town" of Asheville to eat. Mama occasionally took all four of us to a drive-in, one of those fad restaurants of the 1960s where cars pulled up, parked, and the order was called in through a speaker.

Apparently on one of our rides to the drive-in, I wouldn't stop aggravating my sisters, no matter what Mama said. I was in the backseat, out of the range of her quick backhand. Sometimes she used a woman's shoe tree—a piece of spring metal with a wooden toe on one end and a wooden heel on the other—to extend her reach. When I got popped with that shoe tree, it got my attention real quick. But this time, even though she kept warning me to behave, I had no intention of leaving the girls alone.

"If you don't stop right now," Mama said, "I'm going to pull over and lock you up in the trunk." I could tell her patience was about gone.

But I was one of those hardheaded kids who didn't respond to such simple threats. The thrill of seeing the girls squeal and fight me off was too irresistible. Besides, where in the world would Mama pull over on a busy road? I started pinching them again.

"That's enough!" Mama pulled off to the side of the road and stopped the car.

Before I knew what was happening, she opened the back door, grabbed me with both hands, jerked me around back, opened the trunk, put me inside, and slammed the lid shut.

"Can you breathe in there?" she asked.

"Yes, ma'am," I said. It was hard to keep from laughing. This wasn't punishment. It was a new adventure.

"Good," she said, and she got back in the car and drove onto the highway.

I wasn't expecting Mama to drive all the way to Asheville before letting me out, but she drove on and on. I really didn't mind because I occupied myself with the spare tire and the car jack. When we arrived at the drive-in, Mama came around to the back of the car and opened the trunk to get my order. "What do you want to eat?"

"Cheeseburger without the meat, French fries, and a Coke."

She slammed the trunk again and climbed back in the car and placed the order. It didn't take long before the waitress was back with our food. As she hooked the tray to the car window, the waitress was shocked when she saw Mama open the trunk and hand me my food.

I took it, expecting her to let me out. Not Mama. She was determined that I would learn my lesson. She let me eat right there in my own private dining car.

That was Mama. She always took the unorthodox approach to solving problems. And with me she gained plenty of experience.

"Jesus loves me this I know" . . .

WHEN FRANKLIN WAS BORN, Luverne Gustavson, Bill's secretary at the time, gave him a little stuffed black lamb containing a music box, which, when wound, played "Jesus Loves Me."

It is on the bookshelf in my bedroom now beside a picture of Franklin in Israel holding a little black lamb. Prophetic? Almost. A comfort? Frequently.

Fleeing from You
nothing he sees
of Your preceding
as he flees.

Choosing his own paths
how could he know
Your hand directs
where he shall go.

Thinking he's free
"free at last,"
unaware Your right hand
holds him fast.

Waiting for darkness
to hide in night,
not knowing, with You
dark is as light.

Poor prodigal!
Seeking a "where" from "whence"
how does one escape
omnipotence?

Little moth,
whate'er your name,
why do you fly
into the flame? . . .

If I could stand aside
and see him walking through
those Splendor'd Gates
thrown wide,
instead of me—
If I could yield my place
to this, my boy,
the tears upon my upturned face
would be of joy!

I FOUND PARTICULAR PLEASURE on becoming a grandmother to Franklin's son.

God, look who my daddy is!
He is the one
who wore his guardian angel out
(he thought it fun).
First, it was bikes:
he tore around those hills
like something wild,
breaking his bones
in one of many spills;
next, it was cars:
how fast he drove (though well)
only patrolmen
and his guardian angel knew
the first complained,
the second never tells.
Then it was planes:
that was the closest we
ever got—till now,
I never knew him well
except that he
kept that angelic guardian
on his toes.

Not long ago
You touched him,
and he turned.
Oh Lord, what grace!
(And how quizzical the look
upon his angel's face:
a sort of skidding-to-a-stop
to change his pace.)
And now, he just had me:
which only shows
who needs a little angel of his own
to keep him on his toes.
Oh, humorous vengeance!
Recompense—with fun!
I'll keep him busy, Lord.
Well done! Well done!

Franklin Graham on Ruth Bell Graham

Although I probably deserved tougher rules, as I look back, my parents really did give me a lot of freedom. When I took to wearing my hair long—the style by the end of the 1960s, neither of them made any ruckus over it. I was lucky because most of my friends were hassled by their folks about their hair. I bragged to my friends about how "cool" my folks were.

My parents were also really pretty good about giving me liberty to come and go as I pleased. I didn't have a curfew like my friends. I came home at night when I was good and ready—as long as it was sometime before midnight.

But my mother, like most mothers, had her own way of getting her point across. She always sat up and waited until I got home—no matter what time it was. It really bugged me, because it made me feel guilty.

I don't know how many times I tried to slip in late. There she would be, dressed in her robe, sitting in her rocker with a book or a Bible on her lap. "Thank God, you're all right," she'd say. That was it! She never lectured me or made threats.

"You don't need to wait up for me," I'd say sheepishly.

Mama would just smile, say good-night, and go to her room. No matter how I begged her not to wait up for me, she was always there with the light on when I arrived.

As intent as I was on showing my independence and partying late if I wanted to,

after a while Mama's night watchman routine got to me. I began to feel ashamed that Mama was losing sleep waiting up for me. I knew my mother well enough to know that she was not going to change her ways, so I had to change mine. I finally just gave up and started coming home earlier. I ended up with a curfew of my own making!

One morning Mama called me to get up for school. I had been out late the night before, and I didn't feel like budging.

My mother is a very unpredictable woman, and I'm sure I get plenty of my spunk from her. I was half asleep, thinking she had given up on waking me. She quietly walked in my room, grabbed the overflowing ashtray by my bed, and dumped the cigarette butts and ashes all over my head.

"Now get up!" she said.

I jumped up, madder than a hornet. I could hear her laughing as she walked down the hall.

The next night I locked my door. The following morning Mama found a little firecracker of mine in her toolbox, lit the fuse, and slid it under the door. To say the least, I sprang up thinking a terrorist car bomb had gone off.

Mama wasn't about to give up—neither was I. The next morning not only did I have the door locked, but I had wedged a wet bath towel into the crack under my door. I thought for sure I was safe from a firecracker blowing me out of bed. About that time, I heard Mama coming down the hall. I was in bed laughing to myself as I heard her jiggle the door handle and try to push something under the door. I had outfoxed her this time.

But Mama, being the resourceful woman she is, persisted. All of a sudden I heard the window in my brother's room next door squeak open. I slid out of bed and peeked out the window. Here came Mama crawling on all fours across the roof! This time she was carrying a cup of water, which she had gripped in her teeth. I stifled a laugh. She was planning to douse me. Just as she got to my window, I grinned at her and said "Sorry!" and slammed and locked the window. I stood there laughing and making faces at her as she peered into the window. There she was wondering what to do next. She reminded me of our cat with a dead mouse in its mouth, standing at the window wanting to come in.

She couldn't help herself—she grinned, too, in spite of the cup. Because the roof had a steep pitch, now she had to back up on all fours. It was a sight to behold! Suddenly, though, this wasn't so funny. I worried a little about her sliding off the roof, but it was obvious she was quite surefooted and would be okay. I made it to school on time that day, too.

These confrontations with Mama weren't mean or bitter. On the one hand, my parents made it clear what they would accept or reject in my values and behavior. But on the other hand, they never squashed my individuality or demeaned me as a person. They knew much more clearly than I did the pressures I faced being a "preacher's kid" as well as the oldest son of a "Christian legend." I'm sure God gave them wisdom to know that if they pushed me too hard to conform, I might take off running and never come back—not just away from them, but perhaps from God, too.

Ned was our P.S. baby.

At twelve he was a dandy. He liked Italian boots, leather jackets, and girls.

Public school was a struggle, and when he was fourteen, we decided to send him to Felsted School in Essex, England. Ned and I flew to England in the fall. Our last night together, we sat in the hotel room and watched TV, and he briefly laid his hand over mine.

And it came as a shock to feel the weight of his hand and realize it was larger than mine. It was thirty-nine years ago when a thirteen-year-old girl cried herself to sleep and prayed to die before morning. But morning came and she sailed for Korea. Today I'm glad. But now it's tonight. And boys don't cry.

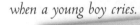

When a young boy cries
in bed at night,
stealthily, silently,
never aloud,
newly away
from family and friends,
too old to cry,
too proud;
too young to know
each night passes on
making way
for a newer dawn;
too old
to stay
in the nest, and yet

too young
to fly
away.
God,
be near
when a young boy cries.

Dear Journal,

Reading again from Exodus 33:12–16. This job of training five little Grahams to be good soldiers of Jesus Christ is too big for me, when I am not a good soldier myself. Feeling particularly distracted (or I should say overwhelmed and confused) this morning, I have been looking to the Lord asking, "Where, from here?"

Bill will be leaving soon for the San Francisco meeting. And I almost have a sinking feeling. Not altogether a left-behind and left-out sort of feeling, but swamped, knowing that all the things I have depended on others to do, I shall have to do myself.

And things have not been going smoothly. There is a terrible amount of fighting among the children, ugliness and back talk from Gigi, and peevishness on my part backed by sporadic, uncertain discipline. (Mr. Sawyer said in speaking of his mother the other day, "When she said 'whoa' we knew she meant 'whoa.'")

I am not walking the Lord's way at all. I am doing what I feel like doing rather than what I ought to do. These verses hit me hard: "She who is self-indulgent is dead even while she lives" (I Tim. 5:6 RSV), and "The fruit of the Spirit is . . . self-control" (Gal. 5:22–23 RSV).

Self-indulgence is doing what we want rather than what we ought. I had always thought of self-control applying to temper or to drink. But what about the almonds in the pantry, the ice cream and chocolate sauce, the candy that I know will add unnecessary pounds and make my face break out? What about controlling my tongue? My tone of voice? Standing up straight? Writing letters? all these and many more need controlling.

And I don't look well to the ways of my household. Children well-taught even to brushing teeth and keeping rooms straight. Regular family prayers at the supper table. Children's clothes kept mended and neat and organized. Getting ready for Sunday on Saturday. Well, there's no use going into it all. It just boils down to the fact that I am not being a good mother.

So I took it to Him this morning. I want above everything to be the kind of person He wants. If He had His undisputed way in me, I would be. Everything would solve itself. The place to begin is here; the time to begin is now. And as I reread Exodus 33:12–16, the phrase that jumped out at me, which I had never noticed before, was: "Shew me now thy way" (v. 13 KJV).

P. S. I could not help but chuckle when I read a quote from Mr. Abba Eban in the *London Times* (June 13, 1980): "Israelis are not renowned for any spontaneous tendency to agree with one another." Neither are little Grahams.

Monday, September 14, 1970

Dear Journal,

For several days I've been bone tired and heavy spirited, easily irritable, negative—just not good company—for God, me, or anybody. Time of year? End of a busy summer? Spiritual recession? I don't know.

But I excused myself early from the kids and their friends last night and went to bed when Ned did.

At 4:30 I awoke and got up briefly but was still so utterly tired I lay back down, praying. In half an hour I felt better, so got up and made a cup of coffee.

And as I sat with Him——reading mainly from the Psalms, just thinking of Him, His love, His forgiveness, His understanding—all the tiredness and heaviness went away. By 7:00 I was refreshed and ready for the day!

Dear Journal,

Every parent should read at least one good book on dog training. Odd how, in a day when children are notoriously disobedient, dog training and obedience classes are increasing in popularity. Basically the rules are simple:

1. Keep commands simple and at a minimum. One word to a command and always the same word. Come. Sit. Stay. Heel. Down. No. (I talk my children dizzy.)

2. Be consistent.

3. Be persistent. Follow through. Never give a command without seeing it is obeyed.

4. When the dog responds correctly, praise him. (Not with food. Remember, don't reward children materially for doing well. Your praise should be enough.)

It is a fine kettle of fish when our dogs are better trained than our children.

Peace in Paris

GIGI GRAHAM TCHIVIDJIAN

It was a beautiful time of year in the French countryside. Large, lush weeping willows dipping their boughs into the Seine as river barges made their way slowly, silently toward the sea.

Our big old house was located on the fringes of a small village about a half-hour's drive from Paris on the Seine River.

Mother had come to visit for a few days, and we were thrilled.

Stephan, the children, and I loved living in France, but being so far away from family was difficult.

One evening, I invited friends to come for dinner to meet Mother.

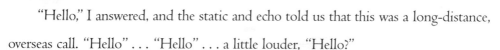

The friends were Jewish by birth, but not religious at all. In fact, they were not sure what they believed. But they were delightful and fun companions.

Early that morning, the telephone rang. I quickly ran down the flight of stairs to answer the only phone in the whole house. It was an old-fashioned phone. To call locally was a hassle, but to call long-distance or overseas was next to impossible.

"Hello," I answered, and the static and echo told us that this was a long-distance, overseas call. "Hello" . . . "Hello" . . . a little louder, "Hello?"

"Oh, hello, is Mrs Graham there?" asked an overseas operator in broken English.

"Yes, I will go and get her."

She came quickly and took the phone.

"Mrs. Graham?"

"Yes, this is she."

"Please hold for Mr. Graham."

Daddy was in Tokyo, Japan. Static . . . static and more static.

"Ruth, is that you?"

"Yes, hi honey. How are you?"

The expression on Mother's face announced to me that things were not all right. But, after talking and discussing it with Daddy, I heard her say, "Well honey, don't worry, the Lord will work it all out. He is still in control. I love you, too. Good-bye."

With that she hung up and told us why Daddy had called.

Franklin, my nineteen-year-old younger prodigal brother, had become engaged. We all loved this girl, at this time also a prodigal, but we felt strongly that they were not right for each other, nor were either of them ready to make a commitment to marriage.

To make matters worse, not only was Daddy on the other side of the world, Franklin was in Nome, Alaska, working for the summer. The girl was in Switzerland studying, and Mother was with us in the French countryside armed only with a very archaic phone system.

What a situation!

All day she was making—or trying to make—phone calls, juggling the time changes and schedules of all the various persons involved.

"Mother, wouldn't you like me to cancel the dinner guests for tonight?" I asked.

"No dear, please don't do that, I'm okay."

Around 6:30, the doorbell rang and our guests arrived.

We did not bore them with our difficult day and the subject never came up. Little did they know. After a delightful dinner of spaghetti, green salad, and garlic bread, we indulged in lively conversation till close to midnight.

Several weeks later, these friends remarked about the wonderful evening spent at our home. But, the thing that struck them most, and made a lasting impression on them all, was the peace that they felt coming from my mother all evening.

Yes, He promises peace that passeth understanding. And what a testimony it was for these unbelieving friends.

Wise and Winsome

GIGI GRAHAM TCHIVIDJIAN

It was a warm, balmy north Florida evening. The waves gently lapped the white sand beach outside of our hotel room and the palm fronds rustled against the window as we dressed for dinner.

Mother was to be interviewed at an event honoring a prestigious medical institution. During the interview she answered questions about her childhood in China, her high school years in North Korea, and then her marriage to, and her life with, my daddy, Billy Graham. She went on to discuss her years as a mother; her joys as well as her difficulties. She talked about the times of having to make decisions when Daddy was away preaching, sometimes tough decisions, alone. She also shared about the trying, difficult years when she had to deal with her prodigals.

After dinner, many came up to speak and to thank her for her honest, open sharing.

I noticed one distinguished, well-dressed woman who hung back, waiting for a chance to speak. Tension was evident and she struggled to hold back the tears. When the crowd cleared, she approached Mother timidly, hesitantly.

"My son died of an overdose of drugs," she said with difficulty. "Do you think I will see him again in heaven?"

Of course, Mother didn't know any of the details, but she saw before her a mother with a very heavy heart. So she answered, "If you heard a timid knock on your door one day, and you answered the knock only to find your child standing there, bruised, wounded, bleeding, dirty, and tattered, what would you do? Slam the door in his face? Or would you throw open the door and welcome him into your arms?"

Suddenly, this mother's face registered relief. I saw the load lift from her shoulders as the tears flowed down her cheeks because she knew she was hearing from a mother who knew what it was like to have a prodigal. They hugged each other, and the woman turned and disappeared into the crowd.

Travel, Politics

BYE, DADDY!

Bill was home more than most people realize, but not as much as we would have liked.

I vividly recall our small, blonde-haired girl sitting in the grass, her translucent blue eyes fixed on a plane overhead and far away. In a wistful little voice she was calling, "Bye, Daddy! Bye, Daddy!"

A plane implied that Daddy was on it, going somewhere. How much we missed him, only each one knows.

THE BGEA WAS NOW AN INTERNATIONAL ORGANIZATION entering remote and troubled areas of the world.

Family life became more pressured, jammed with travel.

I feel like a chicken running
with my head cut off.
Some days I can't run.
Some days I do well to get out of bed.
Here was one year's journey—
Washington, D.C.
England
home
Mexico
Omaha, Nebraska
home
Omaha (surgery)
home
England
Switzerland
France
Germany
home
The Mayo Clinic
home
Omaha
The Mayo Clinic
Los Angeles
home.

Missing the Children

GIGI GRAHAM TCHIVIDJIAN

Mother was not often away from home during our growing-up years. Although she missed Daddy terribly, she felt it her calling to stay home with us children. And on occasion when she was away, we were fortunate to have wonderful friends who took care of us.

Also Mother's parents, Lao Naing and Lao I (Chinese for maternal grandparents), lived just across the street from us, and so we never felt her absences. But, once or twice, she was away longer than anticipated.

Once was during the Harringay Arena meetings in London during 1954. She was gone for three months to London, where it happened to be cold, damp, and dreary.

She was thrilled with what God was doing through the meetings, but underneath she had a longing to see us children. In her journal she wrote, "I can't bear to look at the children's pictures on the dresser, and when bedtime comes, with little more then a quick, 'Dear God, please watch over each one,' I dive into bed and try to fall asleep."

She would write long, detailed letters home and must have revealed some of her longing, because my grandmother wrote back to her in one letter that my sister Anne had prayed, "Dear God, please bless Mommy and help her not to be so homesick for us."

Mother said that she learned an invaluable lesson on that trip. When we are away from God, He misses us far more than we miss Him.

I remember coming home one time and we went to bed. At this time there was a small trundle bed that was under the bed and occasionally one of the children would sleep there. On this particular night, when Franklin was a little boy, he came out from under the trundle bed and saw us together and asked his mother, "Mama, who is that in bed with you?"

Then I began to wonder if she had others in here. I didn't really wonder; I just made a joke of it.

CHRISTMAS . . . a favorite of mine.

"God rest you merry gentlemen
let nothing you dismay" . . .

"God rest you merry,
gentlemen . . ."
and in these pressured days
I, too, would seek to be so blessed
by Him, who still conveys
His merriment, along with rest.
So I would beg, on tired knees,
"God rest me merry,
please . . ."

Those were no ordinary sheep . . .
no common flocks,
huddled in sleep
among the fields,
the layered rocks,
near Bethlehem
That Night;
but those
selected for the Temple sacrifice:
theirs to atone
for sins
they had not done.

How right
the angels should appear
to them
That Night.

Those were no unusual shepherds
there,
but outcast shepherds
whose usual care
of special sheep
made it impossible to keep
Rabbinic law,
which therefore banned them.

How right
the angels should appear
to them
That Night.

"God rest ye merry gentlemen
let nothing you dismay" . . .

AND ALL AROUND ME I FELT TIME SPEEDING PAST.

Oh, time! be slow!
it was a dawn ago
I was a child
dreaming of being grown;
a noon ago
I was
with children of my own;
and now
it's afternoon
—and late—
and they are grown
and gone.
Time, wait!

"Amazing grace how sweet the sound" . . .

Daddy died,
then Mother
and I was alone
on the mountaintop
more than ever.

NELSON AND VIRGINIA BELL

Atop the ridge
against the sky
where clouds,
wind-whipped,
sail free, sail high,
a tree uprooted,
fell and lodged
in the forks of an oak tree
standing by.

The image reminded me of how Daddy
took care of Mother after her stroke.

There they stood—
felled,
upheld,
in the windswept wood.
Atop the ridge
I found them there
one cold Spring day;
and stopped
to stare;

and stayed
to pray.

*Recently, we were out buying flowers for Mother's
garden. She was admiring the lovely day lilies and
decided to purchase several large hybrid varieties.
I suggested that the smaller ones were less expensive. To
which she replied, "No, I want the large ones because
I don't have time left to wait for them to grow."*

I BEGAN A POEM FOR MY MOTHER when I was nineteen—on Mother's Day, 1940, to be exact. I finished it thirty-four years later—November 8, 1974 , the day she died.

As the portrait is unconscious
of the master artist's touch,
unaware of growing beauty,
unaware of changing much,
so you have not guessed His working
in your life throughout each year,
have not seen the growing beauty
have not sensed it, Mother dear.
We have seen and marveled greatly
at the Master Artist's skill,
marveled at the lovely picture
daily growing lovelier still;
watched His brush strokes
change each feature
to a likeness of His face,
till in you we see the Master,
feel His presence, glimpse His grace;
pray the fragrance of His presence
may through you seem doubly sweet,
till your years on earth are ended
and the portrait is complete.

Not fears
I need deliverance from
today—
but nothingness;
inertia,
skies gray
and windless;
no sun,

no rain,

no stab of joy

no pain,

no strong regret,

no reaching after,

no tears,

no laughter,

no black despair,

no bliss.

Deliver me

today

. . . from this.

It must be hard for her to write, but it feels like it just flows out of her without effort. I can see the effort in some poetry, and I don't like to see the effort.

I cannot look You in the face,
God—
these eyes—
bloodshot,
bleary
blurred,
shoulders slumped,
soul slumped,
heart too blank to care;
fears
worn out by fearing,
life worn bare by living;
—living?
too old to live,
too young to die.
Who am I:
God—
Why?

The load
that lay
like lead
lifted:
instead:
peace.
The dread
that hung
fogthick, gray,
faded away;
and with release,
day.
The trial
the same . . .
unsolved,
but this:
now
it is
His.

I awoke to a world
of whitening wonder:
all the bareness of
Winter landscape under
soft white snow
fallen . . .
. . . and still falling . . .
as the dusk falls.
The mountains 'round
are whited out, . . .
and still it falls,
leaving only the nearer woods
etched stark against
the white about.
The only color I can see:
a red bird in a whitened tree.
The only sound in a world gone still:
a towhee on my windowsill.

Such unorchestrated music
one has seldom heard:
dawn breeze
in the tops of trees
much liquid song of bird
sparrow,
robin,

towhee,
indigo bunting,
wren,
meadowlark
and cardinal,
mockingbird,

finch,
and when
my soul is on tiptoes,
filled with ecstasy,
the turkey gobbles loudly
down by the locust tree!

Sitting by my laughing fire
I watch the whitening world without,
and hear the wind climb higher, higher,
rising to a savage shout;
and on my hearth
the logs smile on,
warming me
as they slowly perish:
they had been felled
by ax and saw
while fellow trees
were left to flourish;
but what was spared
by ax and saw,
by some unspoken
cruel law,
was being harvested without
by ice and wind and savage shout.

And on my hearth
the logs smile on.

The Graham fireplace in their first home in Montreat, North Carolina (before Little Piney Cove)

I WAS OPPOSED—ADAMANTLY OPPOSED—to Billy being involved in politics. And I reminded him of this whenever I could.

But there were phone calls from President Johnson.

Invitations to the White House.

Invitations to the LBJ Ranch in Texas.

During the Democratic Convention in 1964, we dined with the Johnsons, and the president asked Billy . . . "Who do you think I should take as my running mate?"

Before Bill could answer,

"Ow!"

A swift kick under the table.

"Why'd you kick me?"

"Because, you are supposed to limit your advice to moral and spiritual issues and stay out of politics."

"I agree with you," Johnson replied. But as we left the dining room, he whispered to Billy, "Now what do you really think?"

Soon Billy became known as the White House chaplain and counselor to presidents.

"Abide with me, fast falls the even' tide" . . .

January 20, 1973, Richard Nixon's second inauguration.

Low gray skies,
clouds
moving fast,
crowds . . .
one man,
and flag
half mast.

THE DAY BEFORE A CEASE-FIRE WAS ANNOUNCED in Vietnam, Lyndon Johnson suffered a fatal heart attack.

For years he made it clear that he wanted Billy to speak at his funeral.

"Don't use any notes," Johnson had told him. "The wind will blow them away. And I don't want a lot of fancy eulogizing, but be sure to mention my name."

Of this historic moment
two things I kept:
that earth was gray
and cold,
and heaven wept.

At the LBJ Ranch Cemetery

Larger than life
he lived here,
smaller than death
he lies
under the spreading oak trees,
under the skies.

If mercy is for sinners,
(which God
in mercy gives)
smaller than Life
he lived here,
larger than death
he lives.

"I once was lost but now am found
Was blind but now I see" . . . .

THOMAS WOLFE ONCE WROTE, "You can't go home again."

But we tried.

My two sisters, Rosa and Virginia, our brother, Clayton, and I returned to our old home in China in May 1980.

I recalled those spiritual giants of my childhood: We visited Uncle Jimmy and Aunt Sophie's old house (now a wholesale grocery outlet), the girls' school where Lucy Fletcher had tutored us, the hospital compound (now an industrial school). So familiar, so changed. Our old home was graciously emptied for our inspection. Behind the welcoming banner stood all that was left—a pathetic reminder of the home that was like an old woman, no longer loved or cared for.

We even located the Chinese house in which I was born.

For me it was like a death and a resurrection. Sentimental feelings for the place, nurtured lovingly over the decades, died. I realized afresh that God's work is not in buildings but in transformed lives.

Buildings fall into decay and eventually disappear. The transformed life goes on forever.

An unimpeachable source had informed me earlier that the Church in China today is both larger and stronger than when the missionaries left. The day of foreign missions as we have known them is a thing of the past. But God, who makes no mistakes, is in control. The Shepherd still cares for His sheep.

An old friend who heard of our coming and looked us up said, "The seed your father sowed is still bearing fruit. Most of the older Christians are dead, but the younger ones are carrying on."

China Roots

GIGI GRAHAM TCHIVIDJIAN

T he jumbo jet eased into the clouds on its descent. My mother, my two sisters, and I had flown halfway around the world for this special occasion. We peered eagerly from the windows, catching our first glimpse of Shanghai, China. A light fog blanketed the countryside. Small, gray-stone farmhouses dotted green fields. Farmers tilled the soil with wooden plows pulled by large water buffalo. In the rice paddies, bent backs were all that was visible as workers planted each small plant by hand. Others threshed wheat by hand, using the highway as a threshing floor. From the air, the countryside looked softly green and picturesque, resembling the many photographs I'd seen.

RUTH (BUNNY), ANNE, RUTH, AND GIGI ON THE GREAT WALL.

The jumbo's tires screeched against the runway. We stepped off the plane and onto Chinese soil for the first time. Yet, in some strange way, my sisters and I felt as though we'd been there before. Something about it seemed familiar.

This was the land of our mother's birth, the land where she had spent the first seventeen years of her life. We climbed into a minivan and began what was to be the first of many thrilling rides in China. Our driver had a unique way of zooming through crowded streets at top speed, never letting up on the horn and seldom touching the brakes. Miraculously, we avoided hitting anyone.

As dusk began to settle that first evening, a little maid came in to turn down the beds and pull the drapes in our hotel rooms. I asked her to please leave the curtains open so I could watch the lights come on in the city. But as darkness fell, a heavy blackness cloaked the city dotted only here and there by a few dim lights. Fourteen million people and so little light. I thought of Exodus 10:22, which says, "And there was a thick darkness in all the land" (KJV).

This verse took on even more meaning as we traveled this great country and discovered spiritual, economic, and political darkness.

From Shanghai, we began a trip that took us to more than a dozen cities in eighteen days. Along the way we discovered part of our heritage and were reminded of the faithfulness of God. We began with a two-day trip by train, van, and ferry, crossing the Grand Canal and then heading north to Huai Yin, where our grandparents had served as medical missionaries for more than twenty-five years and where Mother was born.

On Mother's Day, we awoke to glorious sunshine and deep-felt emotions. We toured what is left of the hospital compound, where God had done so many miracles and changed so many lives. We met many whose lives had been touched physically and spiritually by the faithful missionaries.

I couldn't keep back the tears as I thought of my grandfather, working tirelessly and unselfishly for these people he loved, even giving them his own blood when needed. But he was quick to point out that although he

PART OF THE FACILITIES OF THE LOVE AND
MERCY HOSPITAL IN CHINA FROM RUTH'S
CHILDHOOD PHOTOS.

could help heal their bodies, one day the body would die, so their soul was of much more importance. Then he would tell them of the love of Jesus.

We recalled some of the stories we'd been told as children, stories of God's protection, of His loving care and concern. One Christmas when my aunt was a small child, she had asked for doll baby glasses. My grandmother wondered how in the world she would ever be able to fulfill such a request. But the next box to arrive from America contained—you guessed it—a package of doll baby glasses. How touched we were by the tenderness of a loving heavenly Father who cared about the request of a little girl way off in China.

RUTH AND BILLY IN FRONT OF THE HOME WHERE RUTH WAS BORN.

We recalled another story of two children, a boy and a girl, who were kidnapped by bandits. It was unheard of to find such children alive, especially if no ransom was paid. But God's people prayed fervently, and soon the baby boy was found. A few days later, it was reported that a woman nearby was nursing two babies that were not twins. In this way the baby girl was also found, fat and healthy.

These and other stories taught us that God cares about the small details of our lives as well as the large, seemingly impossible situations that often confront us.

We visited the small stone house where Mother was born more than seventy years ago. I thought of my grandmother, giving birth in that small room with my grandfather tenderly caring for her. I thought of the years of her faithful teaching and living a personal, vibrant faith. My grandparents provided examples of fun-loving Christians, deeply committed to one another and to their work, and totally dependent upon God and His grace and mercy.

I longed to be alone with my mother and sisters to allow all of these memories and emotions to flow. But in China, a country of more than one billion people, it is nearly impossible to be alone. So I thought of how often God told the children of Israel to "remember."

"Remember what the LORD thy God did . . ." and "Remember how the LORD led . . ." and "Remember the days of old, consider the years of many generations: ask thy father, and . . . thy elders, and they will tell thee" (Deut. 32:7 KJV).

I came home to America and my family with a new desire and a new determination not only to be as faithful as I can be in my own life, but to faithfully tell my children of all that God has done and is doing. I want to remind them, encourage them, and tell them again and again of the faithfulness of God.

In China I was reminded again of Deuteronomy 6:7, which admonishes us to teach our children diligently all God has taught us and done for us: "You shall teach them . . . and shall talk of them when you sit in your house, when you walk by the way, when you lie down, and when you rise up" (NKJV).

How important it is to share with our children our own personal scrapbook of the faithfulness of God—the different ways He has led us, provided for us, and sheltered us. Our children need to hear again and again our gratitude to God for His gifts of friends and family and the awesome privilege of freedom. Then they, too, will come to depend upon Him personally, knowing He will also be ever faithful to them.

Remember . . . and tell it to your children and your children's children.

SHE WAS A STREET KID when I first met her in that large city. After she told me of her early years, I understood her present life. She was a baby Christian learning to walk, and like any baby learning to walk—she fell. And fell frequently. Her life in Christ was one step forward, two steps back. Each fall was followed by a renewed effort to follow Jesus. Whenever I was in that city I looked her up. We wrote regularly. The last time I was there, many years had passed. Her once young laughing face was drawn, her sparkling brown eyes, tired. This was written for her.

Perhaps
she will land
upon That Shore,
not in full sail,
but rather,
a bit of broken wreckage
for Him
to gather.

Perhaps
He walks Those Shores
seeking such,
who have believed
a little,
suffered much
and so,
been washed Ashore.

Perhaps
of all the souls redeemed
they most
adore.

FOR THE WIVES of Prisoners of War
and those Missing in Action

Death—
Death can be faced,
dealt with,
adjusted to,
outlived.
It's the
not knowing
that destroys
interminably . . .
This
being suspended
in suspense;
waiting—weightless,
How does one face
the faceless,
adjust to nothing?
Waiting implies
something to wait for.
Is there?

There is One.
One Who knows . . .
I rest my soul on that.

They say
I must not care so much,
or feel so deeply.
I shouldn't study
or read depressing books
like Under the Rubble,
or China Today.
Rather, I should play,
read Agatha Christie,
and relax.
Which would mean
bottling up my
deepest concerns,
turning off my mind,
and growing bored.
But heart and mind
have no faucets—"Hot" and "cold,"
no switch for
"on" and "off."
Cannot one live
with concern,
read deeply,
and still relax? . . .

It seems irreverent
to fly above
snowcapped peaks;
mountains high enough
to earn the snows,
deserve respect;
they were made
to be looked up to,
not down upon,
by man.

Fly humbly,
when you fly;
walk,
when you can.

～

"Satan trembles
when he sees
the weakest saint
upon his knees."
But Satan laughs
without restraints
when saints go clobbering
other saints.

～

Those
splendid, soaring
jagged peaks,
stripped of trees
of grass and sod
on whose snow
the sunlight lingers
are but the Braille
letters, where we mortals
blind and fragile
trace our fingers
to spell the name
of God.

～

Jan Karon on Ruth Graham's Poetry

What Ruth Graham's poetry does for me and has for a very long time (and I hope she understands what I mean by this), is that she makes it feel as if it were my own, as if in fact in some strange way I had written it myself.

I can't say I read her poetry well, but in my inner ear I hear it as coming forth very naturally, again, as if it were my own. I think that anyone who enjoys reading at all (and perhaps they haven't been able to read other poetry because it is too dense, too thick, too veiled) will enjoy her poetry. There is no veil over Ruth Graham's poetry. This woman has had the courage to lay herself bare on the page.

Ruth Graham, married to one of the most famous men who ever lived, is unafraid to let you know that she has suffered. She's unafraid to let you know she feels depression and pain and anguish. I love that in her.

I love her complete openness, her lack of any timidity about showing you who she is. And it's not always a pretty picture. She pleads with God in a number of her poems. It's like, "Stop already." "Please, let this be over." "Give me a break here, God." This is the way the old Jews spoke to God. They conversed with God. "His name is Emmanuel, God With Us," and so often in her poetry I sense that God is right there. She is talking to Him. This is a two-way street.

So, Ruth Graham's poetry is vital to me. It's full of flesh and blood.

Character

Johnny Cash once sent me an old slave collar
from Jamaica. It hangs over my desk.

It hangs there
like an evil thing,
this curve of iron
that round some slave's neck
curled and snapped . . .
the slave long past,
his collar worn rib-thin,
rigid in rust
as if at last
its own rigor mortis
had set in.

RUTH BELL GRAHAM

I WAS IN A COMA FOR A WEEK.

Twenty-five years ago, following a disastrous test run of a pipeline slide we'd built for the grandchildren.

Shattered heel, broken ribs, crushed vertebrae, and severe concussion.

Eventually, I woke up, but the fall planted seeds of future ailments.

Hip replacement, wrist joint replacement, degenerative arthritis in the neck and back.

Spare not the pain
  though the way I take
be lonely and dark,
  though the whole soul ache,
for the flesh must die
  though the heart may break.
Spare not the pain, oh,
  spare not the pain..

SLAVE COLLAR RUTH RECIEVED
FROM JOHNNY CASH

Is the tree that's pruned
preoccupied with pain?
—standing with its wound
in the wind and rain;
shrouded in cool mist,
kissed by the dew,
chosen for a nest
by a bird or two;
enveloped by fragrance
of rainwashed air,
bloodroots and violets
clustered round it there;
gently transfigured
as sap begins to flow—
leaves, flowers,
choicest fruit—
how I'd like to know:
Is the tree that's pruned
preoccupied with pain?

Into the heart of the Infinite can a mere mortal
    hope to gain access,
what with no part of me geared to His greatness,
to His vastness my infinite less?
Yet the longing for Him was so wide and so deep,
by day it crowded life's thronging,
by night it invaded my sleep.

Then came the pain:
again . . .
    and again . . .
        and again . . .

As if a wing tip were brushing the tears
    from my face
for the breath of a second I knew the unknowable,
glimpsed invisible grace.

And I lay where for long in despair I had lain;
entered, unshod, the holy There where God
    dwells with His pain—
alone with the pain of the price He had paid
in giving His Son for a world gone astray
—the world He had made.

My heart lay in silence,
worshiped in silence;
and questioned no more.

All the seasons of my life . . .

Spring . . .

Summer . . .

Fall . . .

When my Fall comes
I wonder
Will I feel
as I feel now?
glutted with happy memories,
content
to let them lie
like nuts
stored up against the coming cold?
Squirrels always gather
so I'm told
more than they will ever need;
and so have I.

Will the dry,
bitter smell of Fall,
the glory of the
dying leaves,
the last brave rose
against the wall,
fill me with quiet ecstasy
as they do now?

Will my thoughts turn
without regret,
to the warm comforts
Winter brings
of hearth fires,
books
and inner things
and find them nicer yet?

Fall's here!

Don't crowd me!
I need room to grow,
to stretch my wings,
breathe deep and slow;
to look about,
to think things through;
Don't hem me in,
don't block the view.
Don't push me;
I need time to grow,
to savor life from day
to day; freedom to go
at my own pace;
leisure to live more thoroughly,
unherded and unhurried,
please; just let me BE.
Don't stalk me.
Follow where He leads
though it may mean
another path, one needs
one single aim in life:
follow well, work hard,
obedient and faithful.
So go!—after God.

A little more time,
Lord,
just a little more time.
There's so much to do,
so much undone.
If it's all right with You,
Lord,
please stop the sun.
There's forever before me
forever with You:
but a little more time
for the so much to do.

BILLY WITH GRANDSON.

Oh my goodness. I'd almost forgotten—

The night
Bill told me
he loved me.
What
did he discuss?
Us?
No.
Emily!

Emily was the girl Billy "almost" married.

Beautiful.
Sweet.
Talented.
Spiritual.
(And second cousin to Herbert Hoover!)
Emily!
I got madder.
(not sadder).
just madder and madder.
till blam!
with a slam,
we rammed
into a truck
(what luck!)
(he was so busy looking back he couldn't see
where he was going. There's a moral here,

but we won't belabor it.)
Still . . .
there were no quarrels
thanks to Charles! (Emily's husband.)

I met her
years later
and knew
I would hate her:
I hoped,
without praying
(that goes without saying).
but I hoped
(how I hoped!)
by now
she'd become
fat and dumb.

Well?
She was a doll!
What's more,
after all.
I liked her!
She'd earned all those laurels.
Still.
Thank you, Charles!!

Charles, Charles, Jr., and Emily Massey

Thus
by the happy twists
of life
folks pair off
as man and wife,
and children come
to bless each home:
> *Gigi,*
> *Charles,*
> *Anne,*
> *Caroline,*
> *Bunny,*
> *Joyce*
> *Franklin,*
> *David,*
> *Ned*

This is the moral
of my ode
(if this is an ode,
and if odes have morals):
Thank you.

CHARLES AND
EMILY MASSEY

THE GROWING MASSEY FAMILY

I met you years ago
when
of all the men
I knew,
you,
I hero-worshiped
then:
you are my husband, now,
my husband!
and from my home
(your arms),
I turn to look
down the long trail of years
to where I met you first
and hero-worshiped,
and I would smile;

. . . I know you better now:
the faults,
the odd preferments,
the differences
that make you you.
That other me
so young,
so far away—
saw you
and hero-worshiped
but never knew;
while I,
grown wiser
with the closeness of these years,
hero-worship, too!

I love these last details of Fall
when past its prime;
the graying hills,
no longer color-crowded, climb,
subdued, to meet a brilliant sky;
when sunlight spills,
filtering through branches
newly bare,
to warm a newly covered ground,
and light the way
for tired leaves
still falling down.
To see a spray of yellow leaves
illumining wet,
rain-blackened trees,
stabs with a joy
akin to pain
that pauses
but to stab again:
when round the corner,
like a shout,
a single, crimson
tree stands out!
After the whole is bedded down
upon the earth's
vast compost heap,

and sight gives place
to faith and hope,
walking up the mountain slope,
lying on my path I find
a last bright leaf
for me to keep.

Barbara Bush on Ruth Graham

I think of Ruth Graham as almost the perfect woman. Perfect because she's got a sense of humor and such family loyalty. And I love her because she says what she thinks. I've enjoyed our friendship.

I've teased her a little bit because I think she has the world's hardest-to-read handwriting. That's her only fault.

I love her support of Billy (I guess maybe that's a generational thing). But to me it is so important to support your husband, your children, and your friends. And Ruth has been very supportive to us.

Tiananmen Square

A still day—
the sky grew dark,
(darkness fell, too, at Calvary)
thunder, like the wrath of God,
shook the earth
as lightning split
low-hung clouds;
then came the wind.
Driving the crowds
walking
thronging
laughing
longing—
Darkness grew darker
the sky grew black. Thunder
came from tanks and guns:
a generation fell under
mindless wrath. Lightning split
power from people.
Brute force hit.
Then came the rains.

To wash away
the Stains?

Beijing, May—June, 1989

The Woman Has a Certain Charm

GIGI GRAHAM TCHIVIDJIAN

"Ruth, where are you?" Daddy asked anxiously. "The Archbishop is due here in a few minutes for tea."

Mother had completely forgotten.

Lunching with friends about an hour's drive from home, she was in the midst of a lively conversation when Daddy called. Being adaptable and spending her life "hanging loose" and "playing it by ear," she quickly excused herself (her friends are used to this, and say that she is a "very loose woman indeed"), got in her car with a friend she had taken to the lunch, and sped off.

After several miles of speeding east along I-40, Mother noticed blue lights behind her. Annoyed, she finally pulled over.

A state patrolman walked up to her window and announced that she had been speeding and he would have to give her a ticket. Impatient and in a hurry to get home, she asked him to hurry and write it up.

He walked back to his car, a bit bewildered, to write Mother a ticket.

When he returned she told him that she was in a real rush to get home and would he would mind driving her friend home since it would be out of her way to do it herself, and also, would he please not follow her because as soon as he was out of sight she would have to speed again.

The patrolman glanced to the passenger side of the car, noticed the pretty blonde woman she was driving home, and quickly replied,

"I would be delighted!"

Patricia Cornwell on Ruth

Ruth and I have always had an unusual friendship. I've always seen Ruth for who she really is. I've never seen her as an extension of her wonderful husband (who is one of the dearest sweetest people you would ever meet in your life). Ruth is independent—a real spitfire—and she's unique. There's nobody like her. You'll never ever find anyone else in the world like Ruth. She's so smart and well read and has a fantastic creativity. I resonate with her wacky sense of humor. I think we have a similar sense of humor. We laugh at a lot of the same things—the absurdity in things. And she's always up for an adventure, whether it's a ride in a helicopter or hang gliding. She broke her arm once when hang gliding and she tried to hide it from Billy. She didn't want him to know she'd been hang gliding because she knew he'd be upset with her. She's so full of life.

The thing that's also so precious about Ruth is that she cares so much about individuals. She cares so much about people. You can judge someone by how they treat people who aren't important. That's the true measure of a human being.

When I was growing up I saw that firsthand. Ruth always cared about us common folk that lived down the hill, no matter who it was (one of the neighborhood kids, or someone who was sick or had a need).

She has never acted like she was better than other people.

Jan Karon on Meeting the Grahams

When I walked into a book event scheduled in Asheville, the manager said, "Mrs. Graham called."

And I said, "Mrs. Graham?"

She said, "You know, THE Mrs. Graham." Then she told me Ruth Graham wanted me to call her. So I called and she wanted to send a car for me and bring me over to their home.

Well, I was beside myself. Some lovely gentleman picked me up and took me to their home and I walked in and she greeted me in the hallway.

She sort of floated down the hall. Here was this tiny, fragile, yet powerful woman coming toward me in her hallway in black tights, ballet slippers, and the most beautiful white blouse I think I have ever seen.

I was swept off my feet by this woman. She had this enormous energy that preceded her down the hallway.

Well, I had driven to Asheville. . . . It's a haul to Asheville, driving up that steep grade and then shaking all those hands at the book event. I was absolutely famished.

And what did she say, "You must be hungry?"

Well I was and I said so. I didn't say, "Oh no, no, no. That's quite all right." I said, "Mrs. Graham, I am just starved."

She said, "I'll be right back." She went to the kitchen and with her own hands made a gigantic bowl of perfectly fresh beautiful fruit—blueberries, peaches, bananas, pears, strawberries. Just the most beautiful bowl of fruit.

Then she brewed tea, in a wonderful ironstone pot, and she brought it all into the living room, herself, on a tray with a glorious piece of starched napery.

And there was a little fire, which I took to be her "laughing fire," on the hearth. And I ate and we talked and I relaxed very quickly. She's very, very easy to be with. She's very accessible. She wasn't Mrs. Ruth Graham at all, she was just Ruth. We just had a lovely time.

And of course I had to ask this question, "Will I get to meet Dr. Graham?"

She said, "Oh yes, I think you will. He's just taking a nap."

I had to really get ready for this, because I felt if I saw him I would burst into tears. He's long been a great hero of mine. I know people who do not know Jesus Christ and who think they do not want to know Jesus Christ, but they love Billy Graham.

Mr. Graham walked into the room and I thought he was the most beautiful man I had ever seen. Because there's that long mane of hair to contend with. And he was wearing blue jeans and a denim shirt. And there's that wonderful hawksbill profile.

And I really did tear up, and I said, "Lord, don't let me make a fool of myself." But there again, instantly he put me at ease.

And so I just sat there and relished this experience as if I had been taken to the very gates of heaven. Dr. Graham and Mrs. Graham sat across from me and held hands. They were so beautiful. I loved seeing them together.

And she was so naughty. She just teased him mercilessly. And he just loved it. They teased each other. He told me about the time in the not too distant past when she'd fallen out of a tree. Well pardon me, but Mrs. Graham really is no spring chicken. She's a mature woman and he was telling me this story about her falling out of a tree.

I just thought they were the cutest, sexiest couple I had ever seen.

The Bake-Off

GIGI GRAHAM TCHIVIDJIAN

M y grandmother makes the best blackberry cobbler in the world," my son Aram's girlfriend, Julie, proudly announced.

"Well, it may be good, but my grandmother's blackberry cobbler beats your grandmother's hands down," answered Aram.

"I bet it doesn't," challenged Julie.

"Well, the only way to settle this is to have a bake-off," answered Aram.

The stage was set.

Several months passed. Aram and Julie fell in love, and Aram decided to propose to Julie in North Carolina during Christmas vacation. He also decided that this would offer the perfect opportunity for the bake-off.

He informed both grandmothers of the event and told them that they had better start preparing.

In Jackson, Mississippi, Julie's very Southern grandmother accepted the challenge. She baked and baked, practicing on friends and relatives till most of Jackson's population had tasted her blackberry cobbler.

In North Carolina, in late December, Aram asked Julie to marry him. She said yes, and the two families gathered to celebrate this special event while the two grandmothers prepared for the much-anticipated bake-off.

In the late afternoon, my sister whispered, "Wait till you see Mother's cobbler!"

Having never been much of a baker, and now in fragile health, I could not imagine that Mother would spend all afternoon baking, but I hoped that at least she had bought a Marie Callender's frozen cobbler down at the local grocery store.

So, after a traditional cheese fondue dinner, we all went to my parents' log home for the bake-off.

The subtle scent of pine boughs and ever-green mixed with smoke from the open fireplace offered us all a warm welcome. The large picture window reflected the tall, stately Christmas tree decorated with white lights and the giant brick fireplace blazed in the warm glow of the fire.

I noticed the special touches. The flowers, the candlelight, the good china, sterling silver, all the things to make this "engagement night" bake-off special. And the aroma of blackberry cobbler wafting from the kitchen smelled promising.

Introductions and congratulations were made, hugs and kisses given, and a prayer of thanksgiving offered. Then came the moment we had all been waiting for.

Julie's grandmother was first. Her cobbler could have easily graced the cover of *Southern Living*. It was beautiful, perfect, lovely. The crust was a golden brown with just the right amount of blackberry juice seeping through the decorative holes carefully cut into the top.

Just looking at it caused our mouths to water. We clapped and sang her praises. Hers would be a hard act to follow.

Mother then arrived with her cobbler. It looked good. It had been baked in a large, black, iron, deep-dish pot. The crust was just the right color of warm brown, and the red juice emanating from the carefully made holes on top looked just right. She approached the two young lovers and presented her cobbler. As she did, she pulled back the crust and there displayed in the dish, were not four and twenty blackbirds, but one very large, dead chicken. His neck had been wrung, blood oozing and falling into his feathers, which were still attached to his very unfortunate body. Everyone gasped.

"Oh my," Mother quickly exclaimed. "Did you say 'cobbler'? I thought you said 'gobbler.'"

When the laughter died down, Julie's Southern grandmother rose and, bowing deeply to Mother, said, "I concede; you win."

JULIE TEMPLE (NOW TCHIVIDJIAN), MARY TODD (JULIE'S GRANDMOTHER), RUTH GRAHAM, AND ARAM TCHIVIDJIAN (RUTH'S GRANDSON)

There Was a Crazy Woman in Front of Me

GIGI GRAHAM TCHIVIDJIAN

The passenger seated in the second row of first class shook his head and rolled his eyes at the flight attendant as he disembarked upon arriving in Charlotte, North Carolina. Still shaking his head, he announced to those meeting him, "There was a crazy woman seated in front of me. She kept tossing things over her head and onto my lap—a newspaper, peanuts, crackers, a brownie, and then more nuts."

Jane Graham, wife of my brother Franklin, was waiting to join Mother on the next leg of the journey. She overheard the remark and chuckled. Turning to the bewildered passenger, she said, "I bet I know who that crazy woman was; I bet it was my mother-in-law."

The rest of the story.

Mother took her seat in the first-class cabin of the US Air flight to Charlotte.

After making sure she was settled, her companion said, "Ruth, I will be just behind you if you need anything."

Mother, taking him literally, threw her newspaper over her head to him when she had finished reading it. Then when the flight attendants served drinks and nuts, she tossed the unwanted nuts back. After lunch was served, she tossed the crackers, cookies, and more nuts over her head to her companion.

Soon, a neatly folded newspaper was slipped back to her between the seats.

Mother became suspicious. Usually her companion threw it away after reading it.

When the plane landed, she was surprised to see that a total stranger got up from the seat behind her and disembarked. Her companion had been "right behind her" several rows back in economy class.

Empty Nest

GIGI GRAHAM TCHIVIDJIAN

"It comes sooner or later to all of us. That is, all of us who have nests," Mother wrote several years ago.

She had just left my youngest brother in boarding school in England and dreaded going home to an empty house.

She recalls entering the front door and looking down the length of the hall and up the steps leading to our now vacant rooms and suddenly realizing that although it was empty of children, it was still full of His presence. She felt surrounded by loving, happy memories and the comfort of knowing that she was home. This was still her base of operations.

She wondered if now she should travel more with Daddy. For two years she tried. Twice she went around the world with him but finally concluded that she "just couldn't keep up with the man." So home is where she decided to stay for the most part.

She wrote, "I want to be here when the children and grandchildren need me. From my vantage point, I can follow their struggles with peace in my heart, knowing that God will bring order out of chaos and light out of darkness. Battles may be lost but God will win in the end. We have given each one to Him, each one uniquely loved, each one dear: our most treasured possessions.

"As each family builds its nest, I shall be watching with interest, and love, concern at times, but concern undergirded with confidence, knowing God is in control."

That was many years, nineteen grandchildren, and many great-grandchildren ago.

Yesterday, my daughter, three of my grandchildren, and I went up to see her.

Yes, this beloved house is still her base of operations. She sits in the large overstuffed chair in the bay window of her bedroom, in full control. The telephone at her fingertips, her Bible open beside her, surrounded by her beloved books, and her walker within reach. (She doesn't let a broken hip, a deformed back, and constant pain keep her down for long. Not long ago I asked her why she walked so fast. She replied, "To get it over with.")

This tiny, eighty-year-old woman weighing in at ninety-four pounds still has her base of operations and is in full control. Loving her Lord, loving her family, and always putting herself last.

No, her nest is not, nor has it ever been, empty. Her children, grandchildren, and great-grandchildren all gravitate to this loving, accepting, encouraging, unselfish, fun-loving, positive, and very spunky little lady that they call Tai Tai (a very respectful term for little old lady in Chinese).

Way Over the Hill

GIGI GRAHAM TCHIVIDJIAN

A few days after Mother's good friend Pedie lost her son in an automobile accident, Mother invited her to come up to her house to spend a couple of days since Daddy was away in California.

"I think that it might help you to get your mind off things," Mother told her.

Pedie readily accepted.

Mother drove down to pick up her friend, who lived a couple of miles down in the valley below. They chatted as they drove back up the long, steep, curving road that leads to our home "up on the mountain."

Mother pulled into her usual parking place, put her car in park, unbuckled her seat belt, and pushed what she thought was the brake. But . . . it was the accelerator. The car tore through the split-rail fence and plunged over the side of the mountain. Mother pushed harder on the brakes, only to accelerate faster through the woods and down the side of the mountain.

An angel must have been watching, because just as they were about to plunge into a ravine, the heavy car came to rest against a very small sapling.

The two women were badly shaken but unhurt. Mother had a phone and called an associate for help.

Maury, their longtime assistant, was beside himself. He went tearing up the mountain road all wheels squealing. When he saw the accident he slid down the side of the mountain, tearing his pants as he went.

"Ruth, Ruth, are you all right?" he inquired anxiously.

"No," Mother moaned, "I think I broke my back and maybe both legs, too."

Maury was horrified, scared to death. After all, when Daddy is away, it was his responsibility to watch over Mother. About this time, Pedie leaned around and winked at Maury.

Mother was just pulling his leg.

Well when his blood pressure subsided a bit, he helped get the two women out of the totaled car and back up to the house where they got tickled. They even admitted that it had been kind of fun! And if Mother's goal was to help get Pedie's mind off things . . . well, it had worked.

But the family was horrified, especially Daddy.

He called from California and stated in no uncertain terms that there would be no more driving for Mother. She would have to give up her license, and they would not replace her car.

Well, Mother, being Mother, argued with him.

Daddy became quite silent on the other end of the phone.

Finally he said, "I don't recall reading in Scripture that Sarah ever talked to Abraham like this."

Without missing a beat, Mother replied, "Well, I don't recall reading in Scripture that Abraham ever tried to take Sarah's camel away from her."

Mother's friends threw her a "we're so glad you're alive" party, complete with singing "She'll be coming round the mountain when she comes" and balloons that read "Way, way over the hill."

No one seemed the least surprised a few weeks later to see Mother behind the wheel of the new car she had ordered.

Memorizing the Language

GIGI GRAHAM TCHIVIDJIAN

Patricia Cornwell, the crime novelist, grew up just about a mile from our home. Since she was a small child, Mother has loved "Patsy" and has held a special place in her heart for her.

Mother was the first one who encouraged "Patsy" to write and gave Patricia her first journal.

The first book that Patsy wrote was Mother's biography, entitled *A Portrait of Ruth.* Mother teases her by suggesting that writing her biography is what drove "Patsy" to murder.

Many years later when the Scarpetta crime series became so popular, Patsy sent one to Mother. Mother objected to the language and immediately penned a note to Patsy, telling her that she did not approve of the language nor did she think it necessary to include it.

Patsy wrote back that it was not she, but Kay Scarpetta who used that language. Mother quickly penned another note objecting as before, but this time addressing it to Dr. Kay Scarpetta.

Time passed, and Mother went through several difficult years with her health. One surgery after another, one physical problem after another. One spring, Mother found herself in the hospital for some weeks. Patsy came to visit.

"Well, Ruth, are you still bleeping out the language in my books?" Patsy inquired teasingly.

"No," Mother replied with a twinkle in her eyes. "Now I am memorizing it."

"Memorizing it!?" we all asked incredulously. "Why?"

"Well," Mother replied, "you never know when you might need it."

Where Are You Headed?

GIGI GRAHAM TCHIVIDJIAN

Mother was at the Mayo Clinic in Rochester, Minnesota. Since we were living in Milwaukee, Wisconsin, at the time, I called and asked her to please come for a visit.

She readily agreed. That morning she was having breakfast with friends in the coffee shop who insisted on having their pilot fly her over in their private plane.

So John, the pilot, and Mother headed to the airport.

Soon they were flying high above the clouds. Not long after, the plane descended, landed, and pulled up to the gate.

Mother deplaned.

I was not there to meet her, and John thought that he should stick around until I arrived. But Mother insisted that he leave, assuring him that I would be along any moment.

Half an hour later, Mother went up to the desk and asked to have me paged.

No answer. So she called our home.

"What city is that in?" asked the operator.

"Mequon," she replied.

"Mequon? I have no listing for a Mequon."

Dumb operator, Mother thought.

"It's a suburb of Milwaukee," Mother explained.

"Oh," the voice said, "that will be long-distance."

Long-distance sure is getting shorter, Mother thought.

The phone was answered by a friend of mine, who told Mother that we were at the airport.

"Commercial or private?" she asked.

"Private," my friend replied.

"Well, they're not here, so I'll just wait."

An hour later—

Growing a bit uneasy, Mother went back to the girl at the desk and asked, "Excuse me, but what city am I in?"

"Minneapolis, Minnesota," she replied.

Mother laughed and took a commercial plane to Milwaukee, where we were waiting to meet her.

We're still not sure what happened, but Mother failed to mention to John where she was going, and John, knowing that Daddy's offices were in Minneapolis, must have assumed that was where Mother was headed.

A few years later, she decided to go and visit my sister in Stauton, Virginia, about a five-hour drive from Montreat.

Mother forgot to get directions from my sister and was unsure of how to go. But she got on I-40 and headed in what she thought was the right direction. Soon, she saw a little car with Virginia license plates ahead of her. *Good*, she thought, *I'll just follow it.*

So she did.

Not until sometime later did she realize that the little car from Virginia was on its way to South Carolina.

Although we have had a few good laughs concerning some of the confusion Mother has had about earthly destinations, it is comforting to know that she's always been quite certain of her final destination.

Outwitting

GIGI GRAHAM TCHIVIDJIAN

With a mischievous twinkle in her bright hazel eyes, Mother has often said to us, "There comes a time to stop submitting and start outwitting." She has done her share of outwitting over the years, and a few times, very few times, she has found herself outwitted.

Daddy and Grady Wilson left Mother and Grady's wife, Wilma, in Paris, France, for a

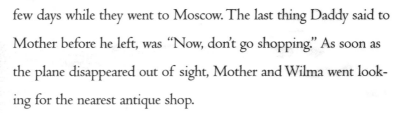

few days while they went to Moscow. The last thing Daddy said to Mother before he left, was "Now, don't go shopping." As soon as the plane disappeared out of sight, Mother and Wilma went looking for the nearest antique shop.

Wilma found several items irresistible, including an ornate silver inkwell adorned with cupids and one or two other items. Mother discovered one lovely little painting for only ten dollars and a little piece of needlepoint that wasn't very pretty but was just the right size for a little footstool, and it was dirt cheap. She also fell in love with a couple of blue-and-white primitive china plates but left them because of their weight, although they were only fifty cents apiece.

The shopkeeper carefully wrapped up their purchases in two packages. Wilma's package was larger, so Mother suggested that when the men got back, she would carry Wilma's package and Wilma could carry Mother's. That way if the men noticed, each wife could truthfully say that it belonged to the other. However, when they got back to the hotel room, they couldn't resist unwrapping their treasures to admire them. Quickly Mother propped her little painting up over the fireplace and Wilma placed her inkwell and other acquisitions on the desk.

A few days later the men returned. After renting a car, they went to the hotel to pick up their wives. Mother and Wilma were busy packing. Suddenly, Mother said, "Oh, I like this little painting so much I think I will just take it home with me." Then she promptly packed it in her suitcase. Quickly catching on, Wilma said, "Well, I like this silver inkwell so much, I think I will just take it." Whereupon, she picked it up and somehow fit it into her suitcase.

A few hours later as the four of them were driving toward Zurich, Switzerland, Mother and Wilma began to laugh.

"What's so funny?" Grady asked. Laughingly, Mother told him about their trip to the little junk shop, their purchases, and what they had done to outwit their husbands.

Silence. Grady didn't laugh.

"What's wrong?" Mother asked. "We only spent a few dollars."

"Well," Grady replied, "it's just that when Wilma wasn't looking, I took the inkwell out of her suitcase and put it back."

This proved to be one of the few times that the women were outwitted.

The Diplomat

GIGI GRAHAM TCHIVIDJIAN

Mother, do you need anything? Are you comfortable?" I inquired, yawning. We had finished eating dinner, and I was hoping to get a few hours of sleep.

"No, I'm just fine," she replied sleepily.

Soon we were both dozing in the cabin of the giant plane as it made its way through the night skies to Hong Kong en route to China and North Korea.

Mother was born in China and attended high school in Piang Yang North Korea. Although on three different occasions she had had the joy of returning to China, she had never been back to North Korea. But in 1997 the North Korean government invited her to visit.

Because the United States did not yet have diplomatic relations with North Korea, Mother asked our State Department for their approval before embarking on this trip. The State Department had been quick to respond that anything Mother could do to open doors and encourage friendship would be much appreciated.

So, with much joyful anticipation, we were on our way to visit this small, unique, charming country where she had spent several early, significant years filled with many vivid memories.

We were not sure what to expect.

We knew the North Koreans to be a proud, warm, and hospitable people, but we also knew that these people had suffered greatly in the past few years. Few Americans had gone before us, so we were unsure of exactly what we would find and experience.

As the plane landed, we glanced out of the small windows. Everything seemed quiet, desolate, dry. This small country had gone through so much turmoil—political, social, and economic, including a recent severe famine.

As we taxied to the gate, we noticed that there were no people at the airport to greet arriving passengers. There were no buses, no taxis, no ticket agents, nothing that reminded us of an airport in our own country.

When the plane door opened, we realized we were the only plane on the tarmac and there was only a small welcoming committee waiting to greet us.

Mother stepped forward, prepared to descend the steps, but suddenly she retreated back inside the plane as if shocked or scared.

We were alarmed. What was it? Was the committee hostile?

No, they were all charming, smiling, and welcoming, but also a little bewildered by the fact that this honored guest had so suddenly disappeared back into the plane.

The reason—Mother thought that her black silk slacks were sliding off and had quickly retreated to retrieve them.

Laughing, we assured her that her slacks were fine. She again made her appearance and descended the steps. After the greeting and picture taking, we all went to a small room for the customary briefing. After she finished answering questions, it was her turn to ask them.

Sweetly, politely, in a very distinguished manner (as a diplomat should), she asked, "How is the health of the great leader?"

RUTH ON A VISIT TO NORTH KOREA.

Maintaining smiles and nodding politely, my brother Ned quickly whispered in her ear, reminding her that he was dead and that his son, the general, was now the head of state.

Still smiling and nodding, not missing a beat, she just as quickly corrected her mistake.

Later, in the car, we had fun teasing our lovely "diplomat."

We were taken to a lovely guest house, where we were treated as royalty and spent a wonderful five days exploring the charming country of North Korea, getting to know her, her politics, and her warm-hearted, proud people.

For the first time, I began to understand the feelings and emotions of a young thirteen-year-old girl sent away from home for the first time.

I understood why she referred to this period as her "boot camp." It was here in this land that she learned to totally depend on the Lord and where He became a great comfort and her best friend.

Years later, she would also send her thirteen-year-old daughter away to boarding school, where she, too, suffered terrible homesickness. But she also learned to rely totally on the Lord and He also became her very best friend.

"Morning by morning, new mercies I see" . . .

R U T H ' S   P R O P O S E D
E P I T A P H

End of construction . . .
Thank you for your patience.

AND SO WE OFFER YOU A VERY FULL LIFE

AND TRAILING IN ITS WAKE

A CADENCE OF MEMORIES

OF JOY

AND OF PAIN

OF BROKENNESS

AND OF HEALING

SNATCHES OF INSIGHT

GLIMPSES OF GRACE

IN THE BRIGHT LIGHT OF LOVE.

THE FOOTPRINTS OF A PILGRIM.

But who lies in this lonely yard
    Where only Birds come too?
Although least the their bodies their souls
        Are with God.
    Up in the Heavens so blue.

Yet here on earth their bodies are dear
    To us who are left behind
And even their frames in their graves
        seem so near.
    And they helps us more - to be king

Yet my mind loves to rome
    To that graveyard back there.
To that are loved ones are - back home
    And when we remember that heart -
I love to think that their bodies are there
    In that small friendly graveyard
        back home.

Yet
But who lies in this lonely yard?
    Where only Birds come too?
At light lies the ~~their~~ bodies their souls
                    Are with God.
    up in the Heavens so blue.

Yet here on earth their bodies are dear
    to us who are left behind
And even their frames in their graves
                    seem so near.
    And they helps us more - to be king

yet my mind loves to rome
    to that graveyard babe there.
To that are loved ones are - back home
    And when we remember that heart-
                    rending care
    to think that their bodies are there
        In that small friendly graveyard
                    back home.

"Where I would love best"